BRITISH WRITERS AND THEIR WORK: NO. 4

General Editor

Bonamy Dobrée

Editor of the American Edition

J. W. Robinson

JOHN DONNE
by Frank Kermode

GEORGE HERBERT
by T. S. Eliot

RICHARD CRASHAW, HENRY VAUGHAN, THOMAS TRAHERNE
by Margaret Willy

UNIVERSITY OF NEBRASKA PRESS · LINCOLN

John Donne by Frank Kermode, *George Herbert* by T. S. Eliot, and *Three Metaphysical Poets* by Margaret Willy originally appeared separately in pamphlet form, published by Longmans, Green & Co. for The British Council and the National Book League (of Great Britain). The Bison Book edition is published by arrangement with The British Council.

Manufactured in the United States of America

PREFACE

BRITISH WRITERS AND THEIR WORK is addressed to the student who wants a general introduction to a particular writer or group of writers, and also to the more advanced student and to the lover of literature who enjoy fresh, thoughtful literary criticism. Each volume includes essays on from two to six writers, the series as a whole being planned to consider British men of letters from the fourteenth century to the present day. The essays in most instances combine the biography of a writer with a critical appreciation of his work. Many of the contributors are themselves well-known English authors and critics.

The essays originally were published separately for The British Council under the titles listed on the copyright page. They are reprinted in the American edition with minor corrections.

It is hoped that not only will the essays prove useful and stimulating, but that the select bibliographies will make each volume a convenient, portable reference work. While the arrangement will vary somewhat from volume to volume, each essay usually is followed by a full list of the first editions of the writer's works (provided as a complement to the account in the essay); a list of collected editions, modern reprints, and student editions; a list of bibliographies and reference works; and a list of critical and biographical studies (including both standard works and other works found especially useful by the author of the essay). Each volume ordinarily concludes with a list of general works. The select bibliographies, compiled by the editor of the American edition, are based largely on the bibliographies originally published with the essays.

J. W. R.

CONTENTS

JOHN DONNE

by Frank Kermode

JOHN DONNE

From a miniature of 1616 by Isaac Oliver. *Royal Collection, Windsor Castle,*
reproduced by gracious permission of Her Majesty Queen Elizabeth II.

John Donne was born in 1572 in the parish of St. Olave, Bread Street, in the City of London. He died on 31 March 1631 and was buried in St. Paul's Cathedral.

JOHN DONNE

I

To have read Donne was once evidence of a man's curious taste; now (though the vogue may be fading) it is a minimum requirement of civilized literary talk. We have seen the history of English poetry rewritten by critics convinced of his cardinal importance. This change was partly the effect of the reception into England of French Symbolist thought, and its assimilation to the native doctrines of Blake, Coleridge and Pater. Poets and critics were struck by the way Donne exhibits the play of an agile mind within the sensuous body of poetry, so that even his most passionate poems work by wit, abounding in argument and analogy; the poetry and the argument cannot be abstracted from each other. And this was interesting because the new aesthetic was founded on a hatred for the disembodied intellect, for abstract argument, for what the French called *littérature*. A series of poets, culminating in Mr. Eliot, proclaimed their affinity with Donne. They also searched the past in order to discover the moment when the blend of thought and passion that came so naturally to Donne, and with such difficulty to themselves, developed its modern inaccessibility. One answer was that this occurred during the lifetime of Milton, who helped to create the difficulties under which modern poetry labours. This very characteristic Symbolist historical myth is usally called by the name Mr. Eliot gave it, the 'dissociation of sensibility'. Mr. Eliot has altered his views on Donne and Milton, but his new opinions have been less powerful than the older ones; and it remains true that to write of the fortunes of Donne in the past seventy years is, in effect, to write less about him than about the aesthetic preoccupations of that epoch.

Donne has been distorted to serve this myth; but it is true that earlier criticism had treated him harshly. As Ben

Jonson suggested, his kind of poetry runs the risk of neglect, especially in periods that value perspicuity. Dryden thought of him as a great wit, rather than as a poet, and a normal late seventeenth-century view was that Donne 'of an eminent poet . . . became a much more eminent preacher'. Johnson's brilliant critique occurs more or less accidently in his *Life of Cowley*. Coleridge and Lamb, Browning and George Eliot admired him, but Gosse, in what is still the standard biography, is patronizing about the poetry and calls Donne's influence 'almost entirely malign'. The revaluation of Donne has certainly been radical. The present is probably a favourable moment for a just estimate. The past forty years have provided the essential apparatus, and though the time for partisan extravagance has gone, so has the time for patronage.

II

Donne was born early in 1572, of Roman Catholic parents. His mother was of good family; and since she numbered among her kinsmen Mores, Heywoods and Rastells, Donne could well claim, in his *apologia* at the beginning of the anti-Jesuit *Pseudo-Martyr*, that his family had endured much for the Roman Doctrine. His own brother was arrested for concealing a priest, and died in prison. His father, a prosperous City tradesman, died when Donne was not yet four, leaving him a portion of about £750. A more enduring legacy was his early indoctrination by Jesuits. To his intimate acquaintance with their persecution under Elizabeth he attributes his interest in suicide (*Biathanatos*) and his right to characterize as mistaken the Jesuit thirst for martyrdom by the hostile civil power (*Pseudo-Martyr*). In fact, his whole life and work were strongly affected by this circumstance of his childhood. He suffered materially; for example, as a Roman Catholic he was disabled from taking a degree at Oxford. But, more important, his mind was cast in the mould of

learned religion. We know that during his years at the Inns
of Court, in the early nineties, he read much besides law;
that he explored many fields and many languages, and—
though described as a great visitor of ladies—rose at four
every morning and rarely left his chamber before ten. Much,
if not most, of this reading must have been theological in
character.

Donne travelled in Italy and Spain, and in 1596 and 1597
took part in naval expeditions. In 1598 he became secretary
to the influential Sir Thomas Egerton; but his secret marriage
to Lady Egerton's niece, Ann More, in December 1601, put
an end to his hopes of wordly success. Her father had Donne
imprisoned and dismissed his post; he even tried to have the
marriage annulled. Donne's dignified apologies prevailed,
but he did not achieve reinstatement, and for some years
lived somewhat grimly and inconveniently in what he
called 'my hospital at Mitcham', burdened and distracted
by illness, poverty, and a growing family. A letter describes
him writing 'in the noise of three gamesome children; and
by the side of her, whom . . . I have transplanted into a
wretched fortune'. He complained, in dark and memorable
phrases, of his hated inactivity. He sought patronage, and
had it of the Countess of Bedford, of the King's favourite
Carr, and of Sir Robert Drury. He worked as assistant to
Morton, later Bishop of Durham, in anti-Romanist polemic,
but refused to take Orders when Morton requested it. The
belated payment of his wife's dowry gave him a period of
relief, in which he wrote more and published for the first
time—*Pseudo-Martyr* in 1610, *Ignatius his Conclave* in 1611,
the two poems for Elizabeth Drury's death in 1611 and 1612.
Biathanatos, which he forbade 'both the press and the fire',
belongs to this time, and the *Essayes in Divinity* were written
in 1614.

When the King had made it plain that he would advance
Donne only within the Church, the poet finally took Orders
(January 1615). In 1616 he was appointed Reader in Divinity
at Lincoln's Inn, where, over the years, he both gave and

received great satisfaction. A learned audience suited Donne, although this one must have been well-informed about those youthful indiscretions concerning which the lack of evidence has never impeded warm speculation; he was accepted as the penitent he claimed to be, and the audience would remember St. Augustine. Donne had found his true *genre*.

His wife died in 1617, her ceremony celebrated by a fine sonnet and a great sermon; Donne was left with seven children. He was made Dean of St. Paul's in 1621, and became the most famous of preachers, invested with a sombre sanctity, and happy in the rejection of 'the mistress of my youth, Poetry' for 'the wife of mine age, Divinity'. In 1623 he was seriously ill, and during his illness wrote *Devotions upon Emergent Occasions*, a series of religious meditations on the course of his disease which is striking evidence of his continuing ability to be witty on all topics; with all its solemnity it has a macabre playfulness and hospital wit.

His sermons are often surprisingly personal; we learn of his family anxieties (the death of a daughter, a son missing in action, his own departure abroad in 1619) and his remorse for past sins. In the end he brought his own death into the pulpit (having wished to die there) and preached the appalling sermon called *Deaths Duell* before Charles I in Lent, 1631. His ordering of the monument which survived the Fire and is still in St. Paul's, and his almost histrionic composure on his deathbed, Walton has made famous. This aspect of Donne has perhaps been overstressed; he and death are a little too closely associated. This can be corrected only by prolonged reading in the sermons, or perhaps by reminding oneself of his marked interest in life: his desire for success, which made him the dependent of the dubious Carr, or his rich and varied friendships—with Goodyere, with the scientist Earl of Northumberland, with Lady Danvers and her sons, George and Edward Herbert, with Jonson and Wotton—many of them central to the intellectual life of their time. But it is still true that he was a sombre man, a melancholic even, and that at a time when this quality was associated with the highest kind of wit.

III

Wit is a quality allowed Donne by all critics, of all parties. In his own time people admired his 'strong lines', and perhaps the best way of giving a general account of his wit is to try to explain what this expression meant. Donne is notoriously an obscure poet—in fact his obscurity is often over-estimated, but he is never easy—and this is often because his manner is tortuous and, in his own word, 'harsh'. Carew's famous tribute emphasizes the strain he put on language: 'to the awe of thy imperious wit Our stubborn language bends'. Carew speaks of his 'masculine expression'; Donne himself of his 'masculine persuasive force'. There was a contemporary taste for this kind of thing, related probably to an old tradition that it was right for some kinds of poetry to be obscure. And Donne was not writing for the many. He expected his readers to enjoy difficulty, not only in the scholastic ingenuity of his arguments, but in the combination of complicated verse-forms and apparently spontaneous thought—thought that doubled back, corrected itself, broke off in passionate interjections. This kind of writing belongs to a rhetorical tradition ignored by much Elizabethan poetry, which argued that language could directly represent the immediate play of mind—style as the instantaneous expression of thinking. And this is why Donne —if I may translate from Mario Praz what I take to be the best thing ever said about Donne's style—will always appeal to readers 'whom the *rhythm of thought* itself attracts by virtue of its own peculiar convolutions'.

Obviously this is a limited appeal. Ben Jonson, himself not a stranger to the strong line, was only the first to accuse Donne of overdoing it. He recommended a middle course between jejune smoothness and a manner conscientiously rough. But for a while 'strong lines'—applied to prose as well as verse—was a eulogistic term; so Fuller could praise those of Cleveland, saying that 'his Epithetes were pregnant with metaphors, carrying in them a difficult plainness, difficult at the hearing, plain at the considering thereof'. But there was opposition to what Walton called 'the strong lines now in fashion'; witness, for example. Corbet's good non-sense poem 'Epilogus Incerti Authoris', a heap of paradoxes beginning 'Like to the mowing tone of unspoke speeches', and ending :

> Even such is man who dyed, and yet did laugh
> To read these strong lines for his Epitaph—

which not only parodies Donne, but foretells the fate of the strong line: it degenerated into a joke, and until recently recurred only in comic poetry. Hobbes, legislating for a new poetry in the fifties, called them 'no better than riddles'. The taste for strong lines is not universal: nor are the powers they require of poets.

As strong lines directly record mental activity, they contain concepts, or, in the contemporary form of the word, 'conceits'. The meaning we now attach to this word is a specialization directly due to the vogue for strong lines. The value of such lines obviously depends on the value (and that is almost the same thing as the *strangeness*) of the concepts they express, and these were usually metaphors. A high valuation was placed on metaphor, on the power of making what Dr. Johnson, who understood without approving, called the *discordia concors*. The world was regarded as a vast divine system of metaphors, and the mind was at its fullest stretch when observing them. Peculiar ability in this respect was called *acutezza* by the Italians, and by the English, Wit. But although the movement was European in scope, it is unnecessary to suppose that Donne owed much to its Spanish and Italian exponents; they were known in England, but they conspicuously lack Donne's colloquial convolution, and his argumentativeness. Johnson's mistake in reporting Marino as a source has often been repeated. Marino has strength, but not harshness, not the masculine persuasive force. We cannot think of Donne without thinking of relentless argument, He depends heavily upon dialectical sleight-of-hand, arriving at the point of wit by subtle syllogistic misdirections, inviting admiration by slight but significant perversities of analogue, which re-route every argument to paradox. Still, in view of the lack of contemporary English criticism on these points, it is wise to learn what we can from Continental critics of witty poetry, and the most important lesson, brilliantly suggested by S. L. Bethell, is that they regarded the conceit of *argument*— making a new and striking point by a syllogism concealing a logical error—as the highest and rarest kind of conceit. This is Donne's commonest device. Of course we are aware that we are being cleverly teased, but many of the love-poems like 'The Extasie' or 'The Flea', depend on our wonder outlasting our critical attitude to argument.

> Marke but this flea, and marke in this,
> How little that which thou deny'st me is;
> It suck'd me first, and now sucks thee,
> And in this flea, our two bloods mingled bee;
> Thou know'st that this cannot be said
> A sinne, nor shame, nor losse of maidenhead,
>   Yet this enjoyes before it wooe,
> And pamper'd swells with one blood made of two,
>   And this, alas, is more than wee would doe.
>
> Oh stay, three lives in one flea spare,
> Where wee almost, yea more then maryed are.
> This flea is you and I, and this
> Our marriage bed, and marriage temple is;
> Though parents grudge, and you, w'are met
> And cloysterd in these living walls of Jet.
>   Though use make you apt to kill mee,
>   Let not that, selfe murder added bee,
>   And sacrilege, three sinnes in killing three.

Cruell and sodaine, hast thou since
Purpled thy naile, in blood of innocence?
Wherein could this flea guilty bee,
Except in that drop which it suckt from thee?
Yet thou triumph'st, and saist that thou
Find'st not thy selfe, nor mee the weaker now;
   'Tis true, then learne how false, feares bee;
   Just so much honor, when thou yeeld'st to mee,
   Will wast, as this flea's death tooke life from thee.

This poem, which was enormously admired by Donne's contemporaries, is cited here merely as an example of his original way of wooing by false syllogisms. So in 'The Extasie': the argument, a tissue of fallacies, sounds solemnly convincing and consecutive, so that it is surprising to find it ending with an immodest proposal. The highest powers of the mind are put to base use, but enchantingly demonstrated in the process.

Part of Donne's originality lies precisely in the use of such methods for amorous poetry. Properly they belong to the sphere of religion (of course there is always much commerce between the two). This human wit suggests the large design of God's wit in the creation. It is immemorially associated with biblical exegesis and preaching, sanctioned and practised by Ambrose and Augustine, and blended in the patristic tradition with the harshness of Tertullian, as well as with the enormous eloquence of Chrysostom. The Europe of Donne's time had enthusiastically taken up witty preaching, but the *gusto espagnol*, as it was called, though associated with the Counter-Reformation, is essentially a revival of what Professor Curtius would call the 'mannerism' of the patristic tradition. Now this tradition was venerated by the Church of England, a learned Church which rejected the Puritan aphorism 'so much Latin, so much Flesh'. And the Fathers could provide not only doctrine but examples of *ingenium*, that acuity of observation by which the preacher could best illustrate and explicate the Word. Donne's youthful examination of 'the whole body of divinity controverted between the Churches of England and Rome provided him not only with a religion but with a style. Some aspects of his Jesuit training would help him in the business of analogy; but primarily the conceit of his secular poetry is derived from his later religious studies. It is, in fact, a new, paradoxical use, for amorous purposes, of the *concetto predicabile*, the preacher's conceit. As usual, we see him all of a piece, yet all paradox; Donne the poet, with all his 'naturalist' passion, knowingness, obscenity indeed, is *anima naturaliter theologica*. What made him a poet also made him an Anglican: the revaluation of a tradition.

IV

It is for this reason that the old emphasis on the 'mediaeval' quality of Donne's thought, though in need of qualification, is more to the point than the more recent stress on his modernity. A great deal has been made of his interest in the 'new philosophy', and the disturbance supposed to have been caused him by such astronomical discoveries as the elliptical movement of planets, the impossibility of a sphere of fire, the corruptibility of the heavens, the movement of the earth, and so on. Certainly, as we know from *Ignatius* and elsewhere, Donne was aware of such developments, aware that it was no longer humanly satisfactory to look at the heavens through the spectacles of Ptolemy. But it is the greatest possible misunderstanding of Donne to suppose that he took this as any more than another proof, where none was needed, of the imperfection of human intellect. Mutability reached higher towards heaven than one had thought; but this only shows how unreliable human knowledge must always be. In *Ignatius*, Donne does not recount the new discoveries for their own sakes, but only as part of the sneering. '*Keppler* . . . (as himselfe testifies of himselfe) *euer since* Tycho Braches *death, hath receiued into his care, that no new thing*

should be done in heauen without his knowledge.' Kepler himself
called this 'impudent', not 'flattering'. When the Devil sees
that he can find no worthy place in Hell for Ignatius, he
decides to get Galileo to draw down the moon (an easy
matter for one who had already got close enough to see its
imperfections) so that the Jesuits can get on to it—they will
'easily unite and reconcile the *Lunatique Church* to the
Romane Church', and a hell will grow in the moon, for
Ignatius to rule over. Sometimes he uses 'new philosophy'
more seriously, to illustrate some moral or theological
assertion. The new astronomy, for example, is 'applicable
well' because it is right that we should move towards God,
not He to us. Or, the Roman Church is like Copernicanism
—it 'hath carried earth farther up from the stupid Center'
but carried heaven far higher. When he wants, for the sake
of some argument, to disprove the sphere of fire, he does not
use the new scientific argument from optics, but the old-
fashioned opinion of Cardan (God would not make an
element in which nothing could live). In serious mood he
often forgets that the earth moves: 'the Earth is not the more
constant because it lies stil continually' (*Devotions*), or: it is
a wonderful thing that 'so vast and immense a body as the
Sun should run so many miles in a minute' (Sermon of
1627). The famous passage in *The First Anniversary:*

> And new Philosophy calls all in doubt,
> The Element of fire is quite put out;
> The Sun is lost, and th'earth, and no mans wit
> Can well direct him where to looke for it,

is merely part of the demonstration of 'the frailty and decay
of this whole World' mentioned in the title of the poem—a
theme enforced by many illustrations taken from a wide
variety of subjects, including the 'old' philosophy. And this
is Donne's way with new or old knowledge. It would be
very unlike him to be much affected by the new philosophy:
'if there be any addition to knowledge,' he says in a sermon

of 1626, 'it is rather new knowledge, than a greater knowledge'. For, if you know as much as Socrates, you know nothing, and 'S. Paul found that to be all knowledge, to know Christ'. There is always an antithesis, in Donne, between natural and divine knowledge, the first shadowy and inexact, the second clear and sure. New philosophy belongs to the first class. What we really know is what is revealed; later we shall know in full.

> Up into the watch-towre get,
> And see all things despoyl'd of fallacies:
> Thou shalt not peepe through lattices of eyes,
> Nor heare through Labyrinths of eares, nor learne
> By circuit, or collections to discerne.
> In heaven thou straight know'st all, concerning it,
> And what concerns it not, shalt straight forget.

V

A mind habituated to such discriminations between the light of nature and 'light from above, from the fountain of light', as Milton calls it, may, in some spheres of knowledge, earn the epithet 'sceptical'. Donne deserted a Church which, as he and Hooker agreed, had mistaken mere custom for law. Liberated from the tyranny of custom, he turns, in his erotic poetry, a professionally disenchanted eye on conventional human behaviour. We may speak confidently of a 'libertine' or 'naturalist' Donne only if we use the terms as applying to literature and thought rather than to life; but it remains true that the *Songs and Sonets* are often (though without his shocking coolness) akin to the franker pronouncements of Montaigne. Consider, for example, his essay 'Upon some verses of Virgil', where he professes his contempt for 'artised' love: he prefers the thing itself, and in accordance with his preference argues that amorous poetry also should be 'natural', colloquial, 'not so much innovating

as filling language with more forcible and divers services,
wrestling, straining, and enfolding it . . . teaching it un-
wonted motions'. This is Donne to the life.

> Who ever loves, if he do not propose
> The right true end of love, he's one who goes
> To sea for nothing but to make him sick.

Donne openly despises the ritual and indirection of Platonic
love; he will follow Nature and pluck his rose (or roses; for
Love's sweetest part is variety). The enemies of nature are
such fictions as Honour; in the good old times, before
Custom dominated humanity, things were very different:
see 'Loves Deity', and Elegy xvii:

> How happy were our Syres in ancient times,
> Who held plurality of loves no crime! . . .
> But since this title honour hath been us'd,
> Our weake credulity hath been abus'd;
> The golden laws of nature are repeal'd . . .

This is the sense in which Donne often celebrates the passion
of love—as immediate and natural, but constricted by social
absurdities:

> Love's not so pure and abstract, as they use
> To say, which have no Mistresse but their Muse.

But of course we must allow for an element of formal
paradox. Donne found this very congenial—it is in a way a
theological, a liturgical device—and his *Juvenilia* contain
such joke paradoxes as a defence of woman's inconstancy, an
argument that it is possible to find some virtue in women,
and so on, worked out with the same half-serious, half-
ribald ingenuity that we find in some of the *Songs and
Sonets*.

> Goe, and catche a falling starre,
> Get with child a mandrake roote,
> Tell me, where all past yeares are,
> Or who cleft the Divels foot,

Teach me to heare Mermaides singing,
Or to keep off envies stinging,
    And finde
    What winde
Serves to advance an honest minde.

If thou beest borne to strange sights,
Things invisible to see,
Ride ten thousand daies and nights,
Till age snow white haires on thee,
Thou, when thou retorn'st, wilt tell mee
All strange wonders that befell thee,
    And sweare
    No where
Lives a woman true, and faire.

If thou findst one, let mee know,
Such a Pilgrimage were sweet;
Yet doe not, I would not goe,
Though at next doore wee might meet,
Though shee were true, when you met her,
And last, till you write your letter,
    Yet shee
    Will bee
False, ere I come, to two, or three.

To take these poems too seriously, as moral or autobiographical pronouncements, is to spoil them; though some are clearly more serious than others.

VI

This may suggest the possibility of dividing the secular poems into groups other than their obvious *genres;* but it is a highly conjectural undertaking. There is a similar difficulty about their chronology; attempts to determine this depend on hypothetical links with events (and women) in

Donne's life. We can say the Satires were written in the nineties; we can place many verse-letters over a twenty-year period; epithalamia and obsequies are datable; one or two references in the love-poems hint at dates. But in these last the evidence is scanty. Jonson's testimony, that Donne did his best work before he was twenty-five, depends on what he thought good—all we know is that he admired 'The Calm' and 'The Storm' (verse-letters) and Elegy xi, a frantically witty poem, but not among the most admired today. Only exceptionally can we say with certainty that this poem is addressed to his wife, that to another woman; this is witty with a stock situation ('The Flea', for example, or 'The Dream') while that is drawn from life. Gosse actually invented a disastrous affair to explain some poems, and absurdly supposed Elegy xvi to be addressed to Donne's wife; another critic has argued passionately that 'The Extasie' is a husband's address to his wife. Even Sir Herbert Grierson supposes that the 'Nocturnall' must be connected with the Countess of Bedford, whose name was Lucy; and a whole set of poems, some of them full of racy *double-entendre*, has been associated with Lady Danvers, ten years Donne's senior and the mother of his friends the Herberts. All we may be sure of is that Donne, with varying intensity, passion, and intellectual conviction, exercised his wit on the theme of sexual love, and that he was inclined to do this in a 'naturalist' way. We need not concern ourselves with dates, or with the identities of mistresses celebrated, cursed or mourned.

The *Songs and Sonets* were read only in manuscript in Donne's lifetime, and so by a small and sophisticated circle. They certainly exhibit what Donne, in the little squib called *The Courtier's Library*, calls 'itchy outbreaks of far-fetched wit'; and the wit is of the kind that depends both upon a harsh strangeness of expression and upon great acuity of illustration and argument. We are asked to *admire*, and that is why the poet creates difficulties for himself, choosing arbitrary and complex stanza forms, of which the main point often seems to be that they put tremendous obstacles in his way. Without underestimating the variety of tone in these poems, one may say that they all offer this kind of pleasure—delight in a dazzling conjuring trick. Even the smoothest, simplest song, like 'Sweetest love, I do not goe' is full of *mind*. Donne would have despised Dryden's distinction between poets and wits. True, some of these poems deserve the censure that when we have once understood them they are exhausted: 'The Indifferent', 'The Triple Fool', and a dozen others fall into this class. Others, like 'The Flea' and 'A Valediction: of my name, in the window', are admired primarily as incredibly perverse and subtle feats of wit; yet others, like 'The Apparition', as examples of how Donne could clothe a passion, in this case hatred, in a clever colloquial fury. This is the inimitable Donne: sometimes, as in 'The Broken Heart', we might be reading Cowley's sexless exercises.

One should here dwell at rather more length on one or two poems. I almost chose 'The Dampe', a fine example of Donne's dialectical wit (the main argument is attended by a ghost-argument, supported by slang double-meanings); and 'Farewell to Love', which would have pleased Montaigne by its grave obscenity; and, for its wide-ranging metaphor and brilliant far-fetched conclusion, 'Loves Alchymie'. 'Lovers Infinitenesse' has the characteristic swerving argument, its stanzas beginning 'If ... Or ... Yet' ... —compare 'The Feaver', with its 'But yet ... Or if ... And yet ... Yet ...' For his best use of 'the nice speculations of philosophy', 'Aire and Angells' and 'The Extasie' commend themselves.

> Where, like a pillow on a bed,
> A pregnant banke swel'd up, to rest
> The violets reclining head
> Sat we two, one anothers best.
>   Our hands were firmley cimented
> With a fast balme, which thence did spring,
> Our eye-beames twisted, and did thred

Our eyes, upon one double string;
　　So to'entergraft our hands, as yet
Was all the means to make us one,
And pictures in our eyes to get
Was all our propagation.

*　　*　　*　　*

But O alas, so long, so farre
Our bodies why doe wee forbeare?

*　　*　　*　　*

　　As our blood labours to beget
Spirits, as like soules as it can,
Because such fingers need to knit
That subtile knot, which makes us man:
So must pure lovers soules descend
T'affections, and to faculties,
Which sense may reach and apprehend,
Else a great Prince in prison lies.

But 'The Curse' is both characteristic and neglected, and 'A Nocturnall upon S. Lucies Day' is Donne's finest poem; so there follow some scanty remarks on these.

'The Curse' has the usual complex rhyme-scheme, and rather more than the usual energy in that Irish ingenuity of malediction which reminds us that Donne was one of the early satirists.

Who ever guesses, think, or dreames he knowes
　　Who is my mistris, wither by this curse;
　　　　His only, and only his purse
　　　　May some dull heart to love dispose,
And shee yeeld then to all that are his foes;
　　　　May he be scorn'd by one, whom all else scorne,
　　　　Forsweare to others, what to her he'hath sworne,
　　　　With feare of missing, shame of getting, torne . . .

The syntactical conciseness of lines 3–5 is remarkable: 'May he win only a mercenary love, yet may he have to spend all he has to get her (and may she be dull into the bargain). Then, wretched mistress though she be, let her betray him— and do so with everybody who dislikes him (presumably a

large number of people).' This only begins the cursing.
'May he suffer remorse, not of conscience because he has
sinned (too noble a passion for him) but because the reputation of the only woman he was able to get makes him
everybody's butt' . . . and so on. The poem ends with an
inventory of hatred and poison, provisions for further
additions to the curse as they may occur to the poet, and
finally—as often in Donne—a light, epigrammatic couplet to
place the poem on the witty side of passion: you can't curse a
woman more than she is naturally 'curst' (forward, fickle,
uncertain of temper) already.

> The venom of all stepdames, gamsters gall,
> What Tyrans, and their subjects interwish,
>   What Plants, Mynes, Beasts, Foule, Fish
>   Can contribute, all ill which all
> Prophets, or Poets spake; And all which shall
>   Be annex'd in schedules unto this by mee,
>   Fall on that man; For if it be a shee
>   Nature before hand hath out-cursed mee.

So much of the effect depends on the control of syntactical
and rhythmic emphasis, on devices like the repeated 'all'
(28–29), on the impressive catalogue, the compression of
meaning in 26 which calls forth the neologism 'interwish',
the formal streak of legal diction, and the minatory solemnity
of 'Fall on that man'—that paraphrase breaks down into
inoffensive jesting a poem that gets its effect by an impression
of qualified but dangerous loathing. This is pure Donne; as a
matter of opinion good, as a matter of fact unique.

This last is true, *a fortiori*, of the 'Nocturnall', which has
the additional interest of involving some of his known
intellectual problems and convictions. The imagery is predominantly alchemical; the argument goes in search of a
definition of absolute nothingness; yet the *cause* of the poem
is grief at the death of a mistress. This is the most solemn and
the most difficult of Donne's poems, superficially slow in
movement, but with a contrapuntal velocity of thought. It

begins as a meditation on the vigil of his saint: Saint Lucy's day is chosen because it is the dead day of the year, as midnight is the dead hour of the day.

> Tis the yeares midnight, and it is the dayes,
> *Lucies*, who scarce seaven houres herself unmaskes,
> The Sunne is spent, and now his flasks
> Send forth light squibs, no constant rayes;
>   The worlds whole sap is sunke:
> The generall balme th'hydroptique earth hath drunk,
> Whither, as to the beds-feet, life is shrunke,
> Dead and enterr'd; yet all these seeme to laugh,
> Compar'd with mee, who am their Epitaph.

That which preserves life, the 'generall balme', is shrunk into the frozen earth. Darkness, which is Nothing to light's All, and death, which is Nothing to life's All, reign in the great world; yet the little world, the poet, is far deader and darker, an abstract of death, an epitaph. The world will be reborn in Spring, and there will be lovers; but he is 'every dead thing'. His deadness is enforced by a remarkable alchemical figure, based on the idea that the alchemist deals in the quintessence of *all things*, 'ruining'—abstracting form from —metals in order to reconstitute them as gold, by means of the quintessence. But this 'new' alchemy, on the contrary, works with a quintessence of *nothing*, privation, and imposes on the poet's 'ruined' matter the 'form' of absolute nothingness—'absence, darkness, death'. Alchemical and theological figures come as it were naturally to Donne; he uses alchemy to push the notion of absolute privation beyond human understanding. The poet has less being than the primaeval Nothing that preceded Chaos, which preceded Creation; he is a quintessence of Nothing: 'I am None.' The internal rhyme with 'Sunne' (meaning light, and All, as well as the woman responsible for his state of non-being) brings us back, at the end, to the commonplace lovers whose activity will be restored in Spring, when the commonplace sun returns.

But I am None; nor will my Sunne renew.
You lovers, for whose sake, the lesser Sunne
At this time to the Goat is runne
To fetch new lust, and give it you,
        Enjoy your summer all;
    Since shee enjoyes her long nights festivall,
    Let mee prepare towards her, and let mee call
    This houre her Vigill, and her Eve, since this
    Both the yeares, and the dayes deep midnight is.

The witty sneer about the object of the sun's journey to the
Tropic of Capricorn helps to distance these inferior loves;
and we return to darkness, the perpetual sleep of the other
Sun, and the propriety of this saint's day as the type of darkness and lifelessness.

This is a brutally inadequate account of a marvellous poem.
My main object is to make a point about Donne's use, in
poetry, of ideas he clearly regarded as important. The
general balm, the alchemical ruin, the violent paradoxes on
All and Nothing, belong to Donne's mental habit. There is,
for instance, a fine examination of the All-Nothing paradox
in the exegetical passages on Genesis in *Essayes in Divinity*s
and it occurs in the sermons. As he extracted the notion of
absolute privation in alchemical terms, Donne must have
been thinking of the Cabbalistic description of God as the
nothing, the quintessence of nothing; here a keen and pre-
judiced ear might discover one of his blasphemies. But it is
more interesting, I think, that Donne the poet is claiming
what Donne the theologian calls impossible; he constantly
recurs to the point that man cannot desire annihilation. So
the wit of the poem (using the word in its full sense) really
derives from its making, by plausible argument, the impossible seem true. And he does it by the use of figures from
alchemy, an art traditionally associated with the resurrection
of the body, the escape from annihilation—he spoke in his
own last illness of his physical decay as the alchemical ruining
of his body before resurrection; here, with vertiginous wit,
he uses the same analogy to prove the contrary. It is not

inappropriate that the finest of the *Songs and Sonets* should also be the most sombrely witty, and the most difficult.

Of Donne's twenty Elegies I have room to say little. They are love-poems in loose iambic pentameter couplets, owing a general debt, for tone and situation, to the *Amores* of Ovid; the Roman poet loses no wit, but acquires harshness, masculinity. These poems are full of sexual energy, whether it comes out in frank libertinism, or in the wit of some more serious attachment. 'The Anagram' (ii) is an example of the wit that proved all too imitable, all too ready to degenerate into fooling—it is a series of paradoxes on somebody's foul mistress, a theme curernt at the time. *Elegy* viii is a similar poem, comparing one's own and another's mistress, with plenty of unpleasant detail. But the Elegies have a considerable variety of tone, ranging from the set pieces on Change and Variety (iii and xvii) which are paralleled by several of the *Songs and Sonets*, to the passionate xvi and the sombre xii, on the theme of parting:

> Nor praise, nor dispraise me, nor blesse nor curse
> Openly loves force, nor in bed fright thy Nurse
> With midnights startings, crying out, oh, oh
> Nurse, ô my love is slaine, I saw him goe
> O'r the white Alpes alone . . .

The Elegies have always had a reputation for indecency, and they certainly exploit the sexual puns so much enjoyed by Elizabethan readers. Among the poems excluded from the first edition is the magnificently erotic *Elegy* xix, 'Going to Bed': too curious a consideration of some of the metaphors in this poem (such as the passage about 'imputed grace') has led critics to charge it with blasphemy, a risk Donne often runs by the very nature of his method. Montaigne might have complained that Donne here substitutes a new mythology and metaphysics of love for those he had abandoned, new presbyter for old priest. But it is impossible not to admire the translation of sexual into mental activity. *Elegy* xix was later regarded as the poet's own epithalamion, a fancy as harmless as it is improbable, except that it has perhaps resulted in the acceptance of a very inferior reading in line 46.[1] One beautiful and exceptional poem is *Elegy* ix, 'The Autumnall' to Lady Danvers; but even this would not, I think, quite escape Sir Herbert Grierson's criticism, that Donne (especially in the Elegies) shows 'a radical want of delicacy'; for it has the wit and fantastic range of reference that mark the erotic Elegies.

The Satires belong to the same phase of Donne's talent as the work I have been discussing. They are, as Elizabethan satire was supposed to be, rough and harsh, written in that low style that Donne so often used, though here it is conventional. *Satyre* iii I shall discuss later; of the others we may say that they have the usual energy, a richness of contemporary observation rather splenetic, of course, in character. Pope thought them worth much trouble, but it is doubtful if, except for iii, they play much part in anybody's thinking about Donne. The same may be said of the epicedes and obsequies, funeral poems which in this period were often, when they were not pastoral elegies, poems of fantastically tormented wit. So Donne proves, in the elegy on Prince Henry, that 'wee May safelyer say, that we are dead, then hee'. The form suited him only too well. The same cannot be said of the epithalamion; Spencer is the poet to thrive here. Yet there are fine things in Donne's poem for the marriage of the Princess Elizabeth in 1613:

> Up, up, faire Bride, and call,
> Thy starres, from out their severall boxes, take
> Thy Rubies, Pearles, and Diamonds forth, and make
> Thy selfe a constellation, of them All,
>   And by their blazing signifie,
> That a Great Princess falls, but doth not die.

[1] 'There is no pennance due to innocence', the reading of 1669, is represented in most manuscripts by 'There is no pennance, much les innocence'. The received reading makes the poem slightly more appropriate if the woman is a bride. But clearly she is no more innocent than she is penitent, and ought not to be wearing the white linen which signifies either innocence or penitence.

Donne could not speak without wit; it is this naturalness that often redeems him.

Of the occasional verse included under the title 'Letters to Severali Personages' a word must suffice. There is a mistaken view that they are negligible because they occasionally flatter. They were written over many years, and not all for profit: notice the little-known verses to Goodyere (Grierson, I. 183) which have the strong Jonsonian ring; the charming 'Mad paper, stay' to Lady Herbert before her re-marriage. The best, probably, are to the Countess of Bedford, dependant though Donne may have been; and the poem beginning 'You have refin'd mee' is a great poem, certainly no more 'blasphemous' in its compliment than *Elegy* xix in its persuasions.

This matter of blasphemous allusion comes to a head in the two *Anniversaries*, written for Sir Robert Drury on the death of his daughter Elizabeth, and published in 1611 and 1612. These are amazingly eleborate laments for a girl Donne had never seen. The first he called 'An Anatomy of the World', announcing in his full title that the death of Elizabeth Drury is the *occasion* for observations on the frailty and decay of the whole world, and representing the dead girl as Astrya, as the world's soul, as the preservative balm, and so on; her departure has left it lifeless, and he dissects it. The second, describing 'the Progresse of the Soule' after death, is similar: 'By occasion of the Religious death of Mistris Elizabeth Drury, the incommodities of the soule in this life, and her exaltation in the next, are contemplated.' From Jonson forward, critics have complained of the faulty taste of such hyperbolical praise of a young girl, and Donne defended himself more than once, though without much vigour; he would have little patience with this kind of misunderstanding. All we may say here is that these poems— now known to be planned in a highly original way as a series of formal religious meditations—are essential to the understanding of Donne; they come near to giving us a map of the dark side of his wit. The death-bed meditation in

the second poem is comparable with the Holy Sonnets on
the same topic:

> Thinke thy selfe labouring now with broken breath,
> And thinke those broken and soft Notes to bee
> Division,[1] and thy happyest Harmonie.
> Thinke thee laid on thy death-bed, loose and slacke;
> And thinke that, but unbinding of a packe,
> To take one precious thing, thy soule from thence.

The *Anniversaries* lead us into a consideration of Donne's
religious life. But we shall find that the poet and the religious
were the same man.

VII

Donne's acceptance of the established Church is the most
important single event of his life, because it involved all the
powers of his mind and personality. His youthful sympathies
must have been with the persecuted Romanists, and his
Satires contain bitter allusions to 'pursuivants', tormentors
of Jesuits; the odious Topcliffe is mentioned by name in some
manuscripts. But he was familiar with the fanaticism as well
as with the learning of Jesuits; and later he decided that the
first of these was the hardest affliction of Christendom,
though the second was to serve him well. No one can say
exactly when he left one Church for the other; it was a
gradual process. According to Walton, he was about nine-
teen when, 'being unresolv'd what religion to adhere to,
and, considering how much it conern'd his soul to choose
the most Orthodox,' he abandoned all studies for divinity.
Donne himself, in *Pseudo-Martyr*, claims to have done this
with 'an indifferent affection to both parties'. Particularly,
he consulted Bellarmine, 'the best defender of the *Roman
cause*' (Walton), and Hooker, whose *Laws of Ecclesiastical
Polity* appeared in 1593, when Donne was 21—though his
famous sermon *Of Justification*, which must have appealed to

[1] A musical term, meaning a variation on a melody, made by dividing
each of its notes into shorter ones.

all moderate Romanists, had long been available. Hooker triumphed; but as late as 1601 the unfinished satirical extravaganza, *The Progress of the Soul*, treats the Queen as the last of a line of arch-heretics, and more dubious references suggest that Donne's recusancy persisted in some form up to the time of *Pseudo-Martyr*. When Walton says he treated the problem as urgent, he is paraphrasing the remarkable *Satyre* iii, which must belong to the nineties. What makes this poem odd is the brisk impatience of its manner, an exasperated harshness proper to satire but strange in a deliberative poem about religion. It has often been misunderstood. The main theme is simply the importance of having a religion; without that one is worse off than 'blind (i.e. pagan) philosophers':

> Shall thy fathers spirit
> Meete blinde Philosophers in heaven, whose merit
> Of strict life may be imputed faith, and heare
> Thee, whom hee taught so easie wayes and neare
> To follow, damn'd?

But which religion? Rome is loved because true religion was once to be found there; Geneva out of a perverse love for the coarse and plain; the English church from inertia. Such divisions encourage on the one hand abstinence from all, and on the other a mistaken belief that they are all true. It is necessary to choose one; and the best course is to 'Aske thy father which is shee, Let him aske his'. Above all, do not rest; no business is as important as this. This is a tentative assertion of the Catholic tradition invoked by all Anglicans —the *true*, not the *Roman*, Catholicism. Donne had in fact to choose only between these two Churches; though he was to develop a great respect for Calvin, he was never concerned with extreme Protestantism. Of the two communions— 'sister teats of his graces' he called them, 'yet both diseased and infected, but not both alike'—he was to choose the one truer to the Catholic tradition as he understood it. Like his learned contemporary Casaubon, he found this to be the Church of England—episcopal and sacramental, but divested of the Romanist accretions. *Satyr* iii is a poem about his search, not about its end. He had still much to do before he could think of 'binding his conscience to a local religion'.

One consequence of this deliberation was that Donne was unusually moderate in later allusions to Rome. In *Pseudo-Martyr* he speaks frankly of its long hold over him, and is charitable to 'all professors of Christian Religion, if they shake not the Foundation'. All his animus is against the Jesuits, for incalculating a false doctrine of martyrdom, and for opening up, by their intransigence, deplorable breaches in the Church. He attacks and satirizes them as enemies of tolerance: 'that Church,' he says in *Essayes in Divinity*, 'which despises another Church, is itself no other than that of which the *Psalm* speaks, *Ecclesia Malignantium*'. Here we are at the heart of his religious position. Donne had convinced himself that Reform had made the English Church more truly Catholic than any other. It was not only a middle way, but the ground on which, he hoped, the longed-for reunion of the Churches might be accomplished. Given tolerence, given an abatement of 'that severe and unrectified Zeal of many, who should impose necessity upon indifferent things, and oblige all the World to one precise forme of exterior worship, and Ecclesiastick policie,' Donne saw a chance of ending the division of the Church.

In this aspiration he was at one with James I, though the prospect of success was much smaller than it had been when the Gallican party in France hoped for something from the Council of Trent. With the King, and his friend Wotton, Donne had expected much of the dispute between Venice and the Papacy in 1606; Wotton, as English Ambassador in Venice, had played an active part, and there was for a while excited speculation about the chance of Venice turning to a sort of Anglicanism. Wooton was aquainted with Paolo Sarpi, the canonist who conducted the Venetian case; and Sarpi's *History of the Council of Trent* was published first in London. In it he deplores the rigidity and extremism of that Council, and, as Miss Frances Yates has said, 'indirectly suggests that if the right course had been pursued at Trent, the Church as a whole would have been reformed somewhat on the model of the Anglican reform'. Wotton sent home several portraits of Sarpi for his English admirers; and it was presumably one of these that hung, as Donne's will testifies, in his study. It was an emblem of his hopes, and Donne completely accepted Sarpi's view of Trent. Preaching before the new King in April, 1626, on the text 'In my Father's house are many mansions', he deplores its intolerance, its coming 'to a finall resolution in so many particulars': as a result the Scriptures themselves are slighted and reduced in authority; and men are the readier to call each other heretics, 'which is a word that cuts deepe, and should not be passionately used'. Both these consequences are disastrous. The priest is ordained to preach the Word—Donne's favourite quotation is St. Paul's *vae mihi si non*, woe unto me if I do not so: 'Nothing,' he says in 1618, 'is to be obtruded to our faith as necessary to salvation, except it be rooted in the Word', and he constantly complains that Rome 'detorts' the Word, as the Puritans do. As for the frequent charges of heresy, he warns his own congregation to 'be not apt to call opinion false, or hereticall, or damnable, the contrary whereof cannot be evidently proved'. Early and late, Donne the preacher insists upon the prime importance of the Word, and on the great need for tolerance; only thus may the Church in England be the matrix of a new universal Church. So, in an early sermon: 'For all this separation, Christ Jesus is amongst us all, and in his time will breake downe this wall too, these differences among Christians, and make us all glad of that name . . .' And in 1627 he prays that God 'in his time bring our adversaries to such moderation as becomes them, who doe truly desire, that the Church may bee truly *Catholique*, *one flock in one fold, under one Shepherd*, though *not all of one colour*, of one practise in all outward and disciplinary points'. This last was after the set-back to the cause in 1626, when the defeat of the Elector of Bohemia elicited from Donne the sonnet 'Show me, dear Christ, thy spouse'.

Donne, then, accepted the Church of England because it was truly Catholic. He rejoiced to discover a Reformed Church which cultivated the Fathers and was slow to come 'to a final resolution' in 'particulars'. He wanted tradition but without its errors: Aquinas, but not the scholastic nonsense; the Fathers, but not their mistakes. The Catholic heritage was enormously more important to him than any 'new' knowledge, theological or physical, and he has little distinction as a speculative theologian, though his age is one of dogmatic controversy. He detested, for instance, the Calvinist teaching on Predestination, which had the intellectual presumption to dishonour God by suggesting that He could 'make us to damn us'; when it was necessary to pronounce on the matter he fell back on Aquinas ('God has appointed all future things to be, but so as they are, that is necessary things necessarily, and contingent things contingently') but he disliked the whole argument: '*Resistibility*, and *Irresistibility*, of grace, which is every Artificers wearing now, was a stuff that our Fathers wore not, a language that pure antiquity spake not.' 'The best men,' he says, 'are but Problematicall, only the Holy Ghost is Dogmaticall.' Though by no means a complete Sceptic, he knew the limits of reason, and often defined its relation to faith (in *Essayes in Divinity*, *Biathanatos*, a verse-letter to the Countess of Bedford, the Christmas sermon for 1621). His position is not dissimilar from Hooker's (e.g. *Laws* I. 8). The limitations of human learning he sets forth in the famous Valediction Sermon of 1619, and the contrast between natural and heavenly knowledge (see the passage quoted earlier from *Anniversaries*) is developed in a splendid passage of the 1622 Easter sermon: 'God shall create us all Doctors in a minute.' Obviously the fierce certainties of some contemporaries were not for Donne. 'It is the text that saves us,' he says. 'The interlineary glosses, and the marginal notes, and the *variae lectiones*, controversies and perplexities, undo us.' He was content with his Church's restoration of a good, lost tradition, just as, in his capacity as poet, he had used a traditional but neglected style that had its roots in the same great body of learning, the teaching of the Fathers.

VIII

No one, then, will read Donne for theological novelties; even in the *Essayes*, which are full of curious applications, Donne's regard for authority puts him at the opposite pole from the radically speculative Milton. And whatever may be offered by the vast array of sermons, it is not that kind of excitement.

It is not easy to give a general account of the sermons. They were preached on all manner of occasions, over fifteen years, and they take their colour from the audience, and from Donne's mood, as well as from the text and from the ecclesiastical occasion. Some were for a great audience, some for a small; some for lawyers, some for the Court; some for Lent and some for Easter; some were preached when the preacher had private reason for joy, some when he was miserable. The tone varies widely. There is truth in the often-repeated charge that Donne was preoccupied with sin and death; he confesses his melancholy temperament (calling it 'a disease of the times') and constantly quotes St. Paul's *cupio dissolvi* (Phil. i. 23), 'having a desire to depart and be with Christ'. 'If there were any other way to be saved and to get to Heaven,' he says, 'then by being born into this life, I would not wish to have come into this world.' There are terrible sermons on death, full of the poetry of charnel-house and worm. There are lamentations for the sins of youth: 'I preach the sense of God's indignation upon mine own soul.' There are even rather grim sermons on apparently joyous occasions; a wedding sermon for personal friends is a forbidding, though orthodox, account of the Church's teaching on marriage, with many gloomy strictures on women. But one can overdo this aspect of the sermons. Death and Sin are fully presented; but perhaps not inordinately. And, to balance them, there is a massive insistence on the theme of Resurrection, and far more humanity than one is led to expect—see, for example, the moving passages on the death of Augustine's son, and that of his own daughter, in the superb Easter sermon for 1627.

> He was but a Heathen that said, If God love a man, *Iuvenis tollitur*, He takes him young out of this world; And they were but Heathens, that bestowed that custome. To put on mourning when their sons were born, and to feast and triumph when they dyed. But thus much we may learne from these Heathens, That if the dead, and we, be not upon one floore, nor under one story, yet we are under one roofe. We think not a friend lost, because he is gone into another roome, nor because he is gone into another Land; And into another world, no man is gone; for that Heaven, which God created, and this world, is all one world. If I had fixt a Son in Court, or married a daughter into a plentifull Fortune, I were satisfied for that son and that daughter. Shall I not be so, when the King of heaven hath taken that son to himselfe, and married himselfe to that daughter, for ever? I spend none of my Faith. I exercise none of my Hope, in this, that I shall have my dead raised to life againe.
>
> This is the faith that sustaines me, when I lose by the death of others, or when I suffer by living in misery my selfe. That the dead, and we, are now all in one Church, and at the resurrection, shall be all in one Quire.

There is no possible doubt that the sermon suited Donne's talents perfectly. That patristic learning which had settled his Anglican convictions and given him his style as a poet equipped him also with the matter and the manner of his preaching; and for the style he adopted he needed all his mastery of the techniques of wit. The preacher's basic duty was simply, as Augustine said, 'to teach what is right and refute what is wrong, and in the performance of this task to conciliate the hostile, and rouse the careless'. This was to be done according to a general scheme which both preacher and congregation took for granted. But within this scheme there could be enormous variation. Donne was of the party that cultivated 'the learned manner of preaching'; not for him the doctrinal plainness of the Puritan. He was, as hostile witnesses put it, 'a strong-lin'd man' and 'a bad edifier'.

How did 'strong lines' go with the preaching of the Word? First: their cultivation did not mean that the Word was neglected. It was stated, divided, illuminated, fantastically explicated. For example, Donne makes much of the expression 'let us make man' (Gen. i. 26): no other act of creation involved a conference; therefore, the Trinity was concerned in this one alone. Secondly: the Word itself gives warrant for all the devices of the learned preacher. The style of the Scriptures is 'artificial'; indeed the Psalms are poems. 'There are not in the World so eloquent Books as the Scriptures . . . they mistake it much, that thinke, that the Holy Ghost hath rather chosen a low, and barbarous, and homely style, then an eloquent, and powerfull manner of expressing himselfe.' The Scriptures use metaphor of 'infinite sweetnesse, and infinite latitude', though they have, when necessary, concision as well as eloquence, simplicity as well as highly-wrought wit. All these qualities are found in the Fathers whom the Reformed Church revived. Ambrose and Augustine—to whom Donne owed most— are ancestors of mannerist wit; Tertullian Christianized the Latin strong lines of Seneca. Nearer in time to Donne was the continental revival of witty preaching, which, as I have said, had much to do with the new poetic wit; but ultimately all depended on the Fathers, and on the wit and eloquence of the Holy Ghost in Scripture.

One famous and passionate page must serve to illustrate Donne's habitual eloquence.

Let me wither and weare out mine age in a discomfortable, in an unwholesome, in a penurious prison, and so pay my debts with my bones, and recompence the wastfulness of my youth, with the beggery of mine age; Let me wither in a spittle under sharpe, and foule, and infamous diseases, and so recompence the wantonnesse of my youth, with that loathsomenesse in mine age; yet if God withdraw not his spirituall blessings, His Grace, his Patience, If I can call my suffering his Doing, my passion his Action, All this that is temporall, is but a caterpiller got into one corner of my garden, but a mill-dew fallen upon one acre of my Corne; The body of all, the

substance of all is safe, as long as the soule is safe. But when I shall
trust to that, which wee call a good spirit, and God shall deject, and
empoverish, and evacuate that spirit, when I shall rely upon a morall
constancy, and God shall shake, and enfeeble, and enervate, destroy
and demolish that constancy; when I shall think to refresh my selfe
in the serenity and sweet ayre of a good conscience, and God shall
call up the damps and vapours of hell it selfe, and spread a cloud of
diffidence, and an impenetrable crust of desperation upon my
conscience; when health shall flie from me, and I shall lay hold upon
riches to succour me, and comfort me in my sicknesse, and riches
shall flie from me, and I shall snatch after favour, and good opinion,
to comfort me in my poverty; when even this good opinion shall
leave me, and calumnies and misformations shall prevaile against
me; when I shall need peace, because there is none but thou, O
Lord, that should stand for me, and then shall finde, that all the
wounds that I have, come from thy hand, all the arrowes that stick
in me, from thy quiver; when I shall see, that because I have given
my selfe to my corrupt nature, thou hast changed thine; and because
I am all evil towards thee, therefore thou hast given over being
good towards me; When it comes to this height, that the fever is
not in the humors, but in the spirits, that mine enemy is not an
imaginary enemy, fortune, nor a transitory enemy, malice in great
persons, but a reall, and an irresistible, and an inexorable, and an
everlasting enemy. The Lord of Hosts himselfe, The Almighty God
himselfe, the Almighty God himselfe onely knowes the waight of
this affliction, and except hee put in that *pondus gloriae*, that exceeding
waight of an eternall glory, with his owne hand, into the other
scale, we are waighed downe, we are swallowed up, irreparably,
irrevocably, irrecoverably, irremediably.

But in addition to such tremendous sentences we find a
hopping Latin wit, as of Tertullian: 'He came, and *venit in
mundum*, He came into the world; it is not *in mundum*, into
so clean a woman as had no sin at all, none contracted from
her parents, no original sin . . . yet *per mundam in mundum*,
by a clean woman into an unclean world.' And we find
enormous conceits and paradoxes. Can man be the enemy
of God, even as the mouse is of the elephant? Man is nearly
nothing, but God is 'not onely a multiplied Elephant,
millions of Elephants multiplied into one, but a mulitiplied

World, a multiplied All . . . Man cannot be allowed so high a sinne, as enmity with God.' But Donne can also be simple, like the parables. So on Irresistibility of Grace: 'Christ beats his Drum, but he does not Press men; Christ is serv'd with voluntaries.' For 'no metaphor, no comparison is too high, none too low, too triviall, to imprint in you a sense of Gods everlasting goodnesse towards you'. To such a preacher the 'metaphysical conceit' was a natural mode of thought. Laud, addressing from the scaffold a hostile crowd, spoke of 'going apace . . . towards the Red-sea . . . an argument, I hope, that God is bringing me into the Land of Promise': here, at such a moment, we have precisely those qualities of deliberate false argument essential to the wit of Donne's poems.

As a preacher Donne is guilty, by modern standards, of pedantry. His style is artificial; he would have been angry to have been told otherwise. The pedantry was partly a matter of fashion, but also a token of his confidence in a truly Catholic tradition. The sermons are inconceivable without it, so is Donne himself. And if he makes our flesh creep, that was still part of his duty; if he almost ignores the ecstatic religion that flourished in his day, that was a defect of his central merit. If we want Donne as a modern poet we may find it tiresome that he was capable of so much archaic quibbling, so much jargon and flattery. But, while it is perfectly proper to read the *Songs and Sonets* and ignore the sermons, it is improper to construct an image of Donne without looking at them; and many such caricatures still circulate.

IX

It was Donne's habit, in later life, to speak slightingly of his poetry; and although he considered, for a brief moment before his ordination, the possibility of publishing his poems, it seems he did not even possess copies of them. There are signs that it was regarded as slightly improper, after his ordination, for 'a man of his years and place' to be versifying, and indeed Donne wrote little verse as a priest. The Elegies on his death often allude to the exercise of his great wit in both secular and religious spheres—'Wit He did not banish, but transplanted it'—but Chudleigh, in these lines, has in mind not verse but sermons:

> Long since, ô Poëts, he did die to you,
> Or left you dead, when wit and he tooke flight
> On divine wings, and soard out of your sight.
> Preachers, 'tis you must weep.

In fact it now appears that the bulk of the divine poems belongs to 1607–15. These years produced the 'Corona' sequence, most of the Holy Sonnets, the *Litanie*, 'Upon the Annunciation and Passion', 'Goodfriday, 1613', and probably 'The Crosse'. The poem addressed to Tilman, the *Lamentations of Jeremy*, the lines on Sidney's 'Psalms', the three great Hymns, three Sonnets, and 'An hymne to the Saints, and to Marquesse Hamylton', which Donne wrote reluctantly in 1625, make up the extant poetical work of the priest. Most of the religious poetry, therefore, belongs to the period of many of the verse-letters, and the *Anniversaries*.

It is verse of remarkable originality. *Satyre* iii shows that even in his youth Donne considered the language of passionate exploration and rebuke appropriate to religious themes; and even when he is working in strict forms like the sonnet, and on devotional topics, we recognize at once that turbulent diction which spontaneously records the pressure of fervent and excited thought. But though he rejected some of the formalities in his secular poetry, Donne was habituated in matters of devotion to certain schematic disciplines. He had been taught to pray; and when his poems are prayers they are formed by this early training. When he undertook 'a serious meditation of God', he tended to do so by employing these meditative techniques.

Here a learned man committed to the reformed religion occupies himself with Papist devotion; but we should not exaggerate the paradox. Donne's Church did not reject what it found good in the tradition; many devotional practises were retained, and some were revived. Donne's 'Corona' sonnets are an ingenious adaptation of an old Dominican system of meditation, based on an obsolete type of rosary called the *corona*. A Puritan might condemn this, but to Donne it was, theologically, an indifferent matter, and good in that it concentrated the devotional powers of a man easily distracted from prayer. More remarkable, perhaps, is the fact that some of the Holy Sonnets, and the *Anniversaries*, are indebted to meditative techniques defined and propagated by Ignatius Loyola and the Jesuits; yet these were so widely disseminated, and apparently so fruitful, that it was by no means exceptional for enemies of the Order to adopt them.

The 'Corona', with its linked sonnets and carefully balanced ingenuity, may strike us as 'mixt wit'; the Ignatian method is more interesting. The purpose of the technique is to concentrate all the powers of the soul, including the sensual, in the act of prayer. So a man might present as vividly as possible to himself the scene of the Nativity or the Crucifixion, or his own deathbed. There is no doubt that this technique, the most considerable contribution of Jesuit piety to European art, affects the Holy Sonnets; Miss Gardner presents twelve of them as a sequence, the first six being formal meditative series on the Last Things. The method is to achieve a vivid image, enforce it with appropriate similitudes, and then to pray accordingly. So, in 'O my blacke Soule! now thou art summoned', Donne imagines his deathbed in the octave, and compares the sinful soul to an exile afraid to return to his country, or a prisoner afraid to be freed; then in the sestet he prays for grace to repent, so that death may not, after all, be like such miseries. The meditation is here forcefully assimilated to the sonnet form, which Donne uses with virtuosity; and the complexities of the form coexist with that sense of immediate and poignant spiritual effort, that tormented natural diction, which was his great, and sometimes abused, discovery. The sonnets are not reports of spiritual exercises; they are the exercises themselves. There is little sense of contrivance, 'artificial' though the form is; Donne reconciles the prescribed form with the true word, just as he reconciles ecclesiastical tradition with the supremacy of Scripture. It is true that the wit of these poems occasionally ventures where we are reluctant to follow, as in 'Show me, dear Christ, thy spouse'. This last complaint for the division of the Church is couched in terms of a traditional image carried to the point where we feel uneasy about its taste:

> Betray kind husband thy spouse to our sights,
> And let myne amorous soule court thy mild Dove,
> Who is most trew, and pleasing to thee, then
> When she' is embrac'd and open to most men.

Perhaps we dislike this metaphor (Christ as *mari complaisant*) because the image of the Church as the Bride is no longer absolutely commonplace; but having accepted the image we are still unwilling to accept its development, even though we see that the main point is the *glorious* difference of this from a merely human marriage. Something is asked of us that we can no longer easily give. Many of the Holy Sonnets have this perilous balance; their wit is always likely to seem indelicate as well as passionate. So in one of the greatest, 'Batter my heart, three person'd God':

> Batter my heart, three person'd God; for, you
> As yet but knocke, breathe, shine, and seeke to mend;
> That I may rise, and stand, o'erthrow mee,' and bend
> Your force, to breake, blowe, burn and make me new.
> I, like an usurpt towne, to'another due,
> Labour to'admit you, but Oh, to no end,
> Reason your viceroy in mee, mee should defend,
> But is captiv'd, and proves weake or untrue,
> Yet dearely'I love you, and would be lov'd faine,
> But am betroth'd unto your enemie,
> Divorce mee,'untie, or breake that knot againe,
> Take mee to you, imprison mee, for I
> Except you'enthrall mee, never shall be free,
> Nor ever chast, except you ravish mee.

This is a great poem, certainly; but what, we wonder, has 'three person'd' to do with the passion of the opening? Yet the poem is another of Donne's exercises in the paradoxes of his religion, and the Trinity is one of the greatest of them. The epithet is obliquely justified by the intensity of the rhythmical conflicts throughout; in the opposition between the heavy 'Batter' and the weak, cadential 'knocke, breathe, shine, and seeke to mend'; in the divine absurdity of Heaven troubling to take the sinner by storm, laying him low that he may stand; finally by the imagery of rape. Love is figured as lust because it is to be rough and irresistible; God is a monster of mercy (but the Scripture compares him to a thief). The powerful paradoxes of the last couplet suggest an infinite series of such: God as infant, God as malefactor, Justice as mercy, Death as Life, and so forth. We respond crudely to this kind of challenge, and such a reading as this is clumsy and over-explicit. Similarly we are inclined to think of a poem that celebrates the coincidence of Lady Day and Good Friday as a toy; but for Donne it was a motive to reverence, a piece of calendar wit that challenged a Christain poet to prayer. We are usually content to be cleverer about the love of women than the love of God; therefore the *Songs and Sonets* keep better. But Donne was clever about both, and sometimes in much the same way; our awkwardness here leads us to charge *Elegy* xix with blasphemy, and 'Show me, dear Christ' with indelicacy. Donne himself was not blind to some of the dangers of his method: in the *Litanie* he writes, 'When wee are mov'd to seeme religious Only to vent wit, Lord deliver us'.

The finest of the other pre-ordination poems is 'Good-friday, 1613'. Here too Donne starts from a paradox; on this day of all days he is turned away from the East. This plunges him onto that paradoxical series where he moves with such assurance; and his wit binds up the paradoxes, with just the neatness and passion of the love-poems, in a fine conclusion:

> I turne my backe to thee, but to receive
> Corrections, till thy mercies bid thee leave.

O thinke mee worth thine anger, punish mee,
Burne off my rusts, and my deformity,
Restore thine Image, so much, by thy grace,
That thou may'st know mee, and I'll turne my face.

Of the poems written after ordination, only the sonnets of the Westmoreland MS. and the three Hymns are of the best of Donne. The little group of sonnets includes the moving poem about the death of his wife, and 'Show me, dear Christ'. The Hymns are justly admired. 'A Hymn to Christ, at the Authors last going into Germany' records a moment of intense personal feeling, and is a companion to the beautiful Valediction Sermon of 1619. The other two belong to the period of Donne's serious illness in 1623, when he also wrote *Devotions*. 'Thou art a metaphysical God,' he says in that work, 'full of comparisons.' And although these poems abjure harshness in favour of the solemnity proper to hymns, they nevertheless live by their wit. 'A Hymn to God, my God, in my sicknesse' is founded on a favourite conceit; the poet is a map over which the physicians pore.

As West and East
In all flatt Maps (and I am one) are one,
So death doth touch the Resurrection.

The 'Hymn to God the Father' contains the famous play on the poet's name (but so does the inscription on the portrait of the author in his shroud, prefixed to *Deaths Duell*); what in our time would be only a puerile joke is thrice repeated in this solemn masterpiece.

Donne's wit, of course, depends on the assumption that a joke can be a serious matter. Wit, as he understood it, was born of the preaching of the Word, whether employed in profane or in religious expression. 'His fancy', as Walton says, 'was unimitably high, equalled only by his great wit ... He was by nature highly passionate.' It will never be regretted that the twentieth century, from whatever motive, restored him to his place among the English poets, and wit to its place in poetry.

JOHN DONNE

Select Bibliography

BIBLIOGRAPHIES

KEYNES, GEOFFREY, KT. *A Bibliography of Dr. John Donne.* 3rd ed. Cambridge: University Press, 1958.
  Contains additions and revisions to the two earlier editions, 1914 and 1932.

WHITE, WILLIAM. *John Donne Since 1900: A Bibliography of Periodical Articles.* Boston: Faxon, 1942.

CONCORDANCE

COMBS, HOMER C., and ZAY R. SULLENS. *A Concordance to the English Poems of John Donne.* Chicago: Packard, 1940.

SELECTIONS

Poetry and Prose. Edited by H. W. Garrod. Oxford: Clarendon Press, 1946.
  A very useful introduction, with notes, Walton's *Life,* and selected criticism.

Prayers. Selected and edited by Herbert H. Umbach. New York: Bookman Associates, 1951.

The Songs and Sonets. Edited by Theodore Redpath. New York: Barnes and Noble, 1957.
  Devised for the student; many useful notes.

The Sermons of John Donne. Selected and introduced by Theodore A. Gill. Living Age Books. New York: Meridian Books, 1958.

SOME COLLECTED EDITIONS OF THE VERSE

Poems, by J. D. with Elegies on the Author's Death. London, 1633.
  Reprinted with various alterations and additions (some spurious) 1635, 1639, 1649, 1650, 1654, 1669, 1719. After 1719 no edition of importance was published until Grosart's, nor was much notice taken of Donne's poems during this period.

The Complete Poems. Edited by Alexander B. Grosart. Fuller Worthies' Library. 2 vols. London: Privately Printed, 1872–1873.

The Poems. Edited by James R. Lowell and Charles E. Norton. 2 vols. New York: Grolier Club, 1895.

The Poems. Edited by Edmund K. Chambers. Muses' Library. 2 vols. London: Lawrence and Bullen, 1896.

The Poems. Edited by Herbert J. C. Grierson. 2 vols. Oxford: Clarendon Press, 1912.
The standard edition.

Complete Poetry and Selected Prose. Edited by John Hayward. New York: Random House, 1930.

The Poems. Edited by Hugh I'A. Fausset. Everyman's Library. New York: Dutton, 1931.

The Poems. Edited by Herbert J. C. Grierson. London and New York: Oxford University Press, 1933.
The standard one-volume text, from the editor's standard two-volume edition (see above), with an abbreviated critical apparatus and a new introduction. Frequently reprinted.

The Complete Poems. Edited by Roger E. Bennett. Chicago: Packard, 1942.

Complete Poetry and Selected Prose. Edited by Charles M. Coffin. New York: Modern Library, 1952.

The Divine Poems. Edited by Helen Gardner. Oxford: Clarendon Press, 1952.
The standard edition of the divine poems.

COLLECTED EDITIONS OF THE PROSE

The Works of John Donne. Edited by Henry Alford. 6 vols. London: Parker, 1839.
Reprints, inaccurately, most of the sermons, some letters, and *Devotions*.

The Sermons of John Donne. Edited by Evelyn M. Simpson and George R. Potter. 10 vols. Berkeley and Los Angeles: University of California Press, 1953–1962.
The standard edition.

SEPARATE WORKS

Dates of original editions are given, and some modern editions and facsimiles are also recorded here.

VERSE

An Anatomy of the World. London, 1611.

The First Anniversary, An Anatomy of the World: The Second Anniversary, Of the Progress of the Soul. London, 1612.
Ᏸ A facsimile of the 1621 edition was published in the Noel Douglas Replicas series (London: Noel Douglas, 1927), and in the English Replicas series (New York: Payson and Clarke, 1927); edited by Frank Manley (Baltimore: Johns Hopkins Press, 1963).

Poems, by J. D. with Elegies on the Author's Death. London, 1633.

PROSE

Pseudo-Martyr. London, 1610.

Conclave Ignati. London, 1611.

Ignatius his Conclave: or, his Inthronisation in a late Election in Hell. London, 1611.
Ᏸ Reprinted in Hayward, *Complete Poetry and Selected Prose* (see above). A facsimile was edited by Charles M. Coffin for the Facsimile Text Society (New York: Columbia University Press, 1941).

Devotions upon Emergent Occasions, and Several Steps in my Sickness. London, 1624.
Ᏸ Edited by John Sparrow (Cambridge: University Press, 1923); edited by William H. Draper for the Abbey Classics (London: Simpkin, 1925).

Juvenilia: or Certain Paradoxes and Problems. London, 1633.
Ᏸ Edited by Geoffrey Keynes (London: Nonesuch Press, 1923). A facsimile of the 1633 edition was edited by Roger E. Bennett for the Facsimile Text Society (New York: Columbia University Press, 1936).

Biathanatos: A Declaration of that Paradox, or Thesis, that Self-Homicide is not so Naturally Sin, that it may never be Otherwise. London, 1647.
Ᏸ A facsimile edition was edited by J. William Hebel (New York: Facsimile Text Society, 1930).

The Courtier's Library, or Catalogus Librorum Aulicorum Incomparabilium, et non Vendibilium. Edited by Evelyn M. Simpson. London: Nonesuch Press, 1930.
Ᏸ First published in the 1650 edition of *Poems*.

Essays in Divinity. London, 1651.
Ᏸ Edited by Augustus Jessop (London: Tupling, 1855); and by Evelyn M. Simpson (Oxford: Clarendon Press, 1952).

Letters to Several Persons of Honour. London, 1651.

A Collection of Letters. Made by Sir Tobie Mathews, Kt. London, 1660.

GOSSE, EDMUND. *The Life and Letters of John Donne.* 2 vols. London: Heineman, 1899.

This and the following work contain many letters not previously printed. There is no thorough edition of Donne's letters.

SIMPSON, EVEYLN M. *A Study of the Prose Works of John Donne.* Oxford: Clarendon Press, 1924; 2nd ed., 1948.

SERMONS

Six sermons were separately published—and collected successively as *Three Sermons* (London, 1623), *Four Sermons* (London, 1625), *Five Sermons* (London, 1626) during Donne's lifetime. *Death's Duel* appeared separately (London, 1632), and the "Sermon of Valediction" (preached 1619) in *Sapientia Clamitans* (London, 1638).

Six Sermons Upon Several Occasions. Cambridge, 1634.

LXXX Sermons. London, 1640.

Fifty Sermons. London, 1649.

XXVI Sermons. London, 1660.

Actually twenty-three, as two are printed twice and one left out.

Sermon on Psalm 38, v. 9. Now first Printed. London: Privately Printed, 1921.

Reprinted (in the first edition only) of Simpson, *A Study of the Prose Works of John Donne* (see above); edited by George R. Potter (Stanford: Stanford University Press, 1945).

RECORDINGS

Poems. ARGO RG 24. Read by Christopher Hassall.

The Poetry. Ann Arbor: Idiom Recording Co. El LKC 3266–3271. Read by Austin Warren.

Sermons and Meditations. Caedmon TC 1051. Read by Herbert Marshall.

Love Poems. Caedmon TC 1141. Read by Richard Burton.

BIOGRAPHICAL AND CRITICAL STUDIES OF DONNE

JESSOP, AUGUSTUS. *John Donne.* Boston and New York: Houghton Mifflin, 1897.

GOSSE, EDMUND. *The Life and Letters of John Donne.* 2 vols. London: Heineman, 1899.

Much new information has become available since Gosse's inaccurate work. There is no reliable full-scale life of Donne.

RAMSAY, MARY PATON. *Les Doctrines Médiévales chez Donne*. New York: Oxford University Press, 1917; 2ᵉ ed., 1924.
An indispensable work.

BREDVOLD, L. I. "The Naturalism of Donne in Relation to Some Renaissance Traditions," *Journal of English and Germanic Philology*, XXII (1923).

SIMPSON, EVELYN M. *A Study of the Prose Works of John Donne*. Oxford: Clarendon Press, 1924; 2nd ed., 1948.
Includes the most complete and reliable summary of the facts of Donne's life.

FAUSSET, HUGH I'A. *John Donne: A Study in Discord*. London: Jonathan Cape, 1924.

BREDVOLD, L. I. "The Religious Thought of Donne in Relation to Medieval and later Traditions," *Studies in Shakespeare, Milton, and Donne*. University of Michigan Publications, Language and Literature No. 1. Ann Arbor: University of Michigan Press, 1925.

LEGOUIS, PIERRE. *Donne the Craftsman*. Paris: Didier, 1928; New York: Russell and Russell, 1962.

WILLIAMSON, GEORGE. *The Donne Tradition*. Cambridge: Harvard University Press, 1930.

SPENCER, THEODORE, ed. *A Garland for John Donne*. Cambridge: Harvard University Press, 1931.
Contains, *inter alia*, important essays by T. S. Eliot, Mario Praz, and John Sparrow.

MITCHELL, WILLIAM FRASER. *English Pulpit Oratory from Andrewes to Tillotson*. New York: Macmillan, 1932.
An important book not only on the sermons but on the history of the conceit.

WILLIAMSON, GEORGE. "The Libertine Donne: Comments on 'Biathanatos,'" *Philological Quarterly*, XIII (1934).

———. "Strong Lines," *English Studies*, XVIII (1936).

CROFTS, J. E. V. "John Donne," *Essays and Studies by Members of the English Association*, XXII (1937).
Reprinted in Helen Gardner, ed., *John Donne: A Collection of Critical Essays* (see below).

COFFIN, CHARLES M. *John Donne and the New Philosophy*. New York: Columbia University Press, 1937; Humanities Press, 1958.

LEWIS, C. S. "Donne and Love Poetry in the Seventeenth Century," *Seventeenth Century Studies Presented to Sir Herbert Grierson*. Oxford: Clarendon Press, 1938.

BENNETT, JOAN. "The Love Poetry of John Donne," *Seventeenth Century Studies Presented to Sir Herbert Grierson*. Oxford: Clarendon Press, 1938.

HUSAIN, ITRAT. *Dogmatic and Mystical Theology of John Donne*. New York: Macmillan, 1938.

RUGOFF, MILTON A. *Donne's Imagery*. New York: Corporate Press, 1939; Russell and Russell, 1962.

DUNCAN, E. H. "Donne's Alchemical Figures," *ELH*, IX (1942).

MOLONEY, MICHAEL F. *John Donne: His Flight from Mediaevalism*. Urbana: University of Illinois Press, 1944.

YATES, FRANCIS A. "Paolo Sarpi's 'History of the Council of Trent,'" *Journal of the Warburg and Courtauld Institutes*, VII (1944).
Shows Donne's connection with the movement for the union of the Church. See also Francis Yates, *The French Academies of the Sixteenth Century* (London: Warburg Institute, 1947), especially Chapter X.

LEISHMAN, JAMES B. *The Monarch of Wit*. London: Hutchinson's University Library, 1951; rev. ed., 1955; 5th ed., 1962.
A valuable introduction.

GRANSDEN, K. W. *John Donne*. New York: Longmans, Green, 1954.

HUNT, CLAY. *Donne's Poetry: Essays in Literary Analysis*. New Haven: Yale University Press, 1954.

PRAZ, MARIO. *John Donne*. Turin: S.A.I.E., 1958.
In Italian.

BALD, ROBERT CECIL. *Donne and the Drurys*. Cambridge: University Press, 1959.

TILLOTSON, KATHLEEN. "Donne's Poetry in the Nineteenth Century," *Elizabethan and Jacobean Studies Presented to Frank Percy Wilson*. Oxford: Clarendon Press, 1959.

SMITH, A. J. "Donne in his Time: A Reading of 'The Extasie,'" *Revista di Letterature Moderne e Comparete*, X (1957).

———. "The Metaphysic of Love," *Review of English Studies*, IX (N.S.) (1958).

GARDNER, HELEN. "The Argument about 'The Ecstacy,'" *Elizabethan and Jacobean Studies Presented to Frank Percy Wilson*. Oxford: Clarendon Press, 1959.

HUGHES, M. Y. "Some of Donne's 'Ecstacies,' " *PMLA*, LXXV (1960).

The last four items all relate to a long-standing controversy about the interpretation of "The Extasie," but the issues they raise are of more general significance.

MUELLER, WILLIAM R. *John Donne: Preacher*. Princeton: Princeton University Press, 1962.

UNGER, LEONARD. *Donne's Poetry and Modern Criticism*. New York: Russell and Russell, 1962.

STEIN, ARNOLD. *John Donne's Lyrics: The Eloquence of Action*. Minneapolis: University of Minnesota Press, 1962.

GARDNER, HELEN, ed. *John Donne: A Collection of Critical Essays*. Englewood Cliffs, N. J.: Prentice-Hall, 1962.

A convenient collection of thirteen important essays, from 1896 to 1960.

WEBBER, JOAN. *Contrary Music: The Prose Style of John Donne*. Madison: University of Wisconsin Press, 1963.

GEORGE HERBERT

by T. S. Eliot

GEORGE HERBERT

After an engraving by R. White which first appeared in Izaac Walton's
Life, 1670, and in the 1674 edition of *The Temple.*

George Herbert was born at Montgomery Castle on 3 April 1593. He died on 3 March 1633 and was buried at Bemerton, Wiltshire.

GEORGE HERBERT

I

THE family background of a man of genius is always of interest. It may show evidence of powers which blaze forth in one member, or it may show no promise of superiority of any kind. Or it may, like that of George Herbert, show distinction of a very different order. There is a further reason for knowing something of the ancestry of George Herbert: it is of interest to us because it was important to him.

The family of Herbert was, and still is, notable among the British aristocracy. I say British rather than English, because one branch of the family, that to which the poet belonged, had established itself in Wales and had intermarried with Welsh landed families. The Herberts lay claim to being of Norman-French origin, and to having been land-holders since the Norman conquest. At the time of the Wars of the Roses the Herberts of Wales had supported the Yorkist cause; but after the battle of Bosworth they transferred their allegiance to the new monarch, the Lancastrian Henry Tudor, himself a Welshman on his father's side, who ascended the throne as Henry VII. Under the new dynasty the Herberts continued to flourish. Henry VII was determined to exert in Wales the same authority that he enjoyed in England—a control to which the local chieftains of Wales were not accustomed. Among those Welshmen of position and authority who supported and advanced King Henry's law and order in Wales was Sir Richard Herbert of Montgomery Castle. Montgomery lies in North Wales; in the South another Herbert was (and is) Earl of Pembroke; and still another branch of the family is represented by the Earl of Carnarvon.

George Herbert's ancestors and kinsmen were active both in the service of the King and in local affairs. Their rank was among the highest. Several of the family were distinguished for their courage, their prowess in war and duel and their astonishing feats of arms. An exceptional race, but giving no indication of literary tastes and ability before the time of George Herbert and his brother Edward. That two poets, brothers, should appear in a family so conspicuous for warlike deeds, administrative gifts and attendance at Court, can only be accounted for by the fact that their mother, the wife of Sir Richard Herbert of Montgomery, was a woman of literary tastes and of strong character and of exceptional gifts of mind as well as beauty and charm. She was Magdalen, daughter and heiress of Sir Richard Newport, a wealthy landowner in Shropshire.

George Herbert was born in 1593. Three years later his father died, leaving the mother with ten children, seven boys and three girls. Edward was the eldest son; the younger sons would have, of course, to make their own way in life—presumably, as other Herberts had done, in the wars or in some public service—but Lady Herbert's standards were high and she was determined to give them all a good education. The eldest, Edward, the other poet of the family and the heir to the estates, was thirteen and already an undergraduate at Oxford when his father died. At fifteen Edward was married off to an heiress (a Herbert of another branch) but continued at Oxford, where his mother moved her family to be near him and to supervise his education. There she made friends, and even held a kind of salon, among the more brilliant of the learned dons.

It is worth while to say something of Edward Herbert, the eldest brother, not merely to mention his poetry but to point the striking contrast between the two gifted brothers. Edward was ambitious to live abroad, to enjoy court life in foreign capitals and to engage in rather dilletante diplomacy; and to this end he learned French, Italian and Spanish. He seems to have been a man of great physical strength, and was noted for his address at sports and success in love-making: in short, he was a man of abounding vitality. He was later raised to the peerage as Lord Herbert of Cherbury, by which name he is known as author of at least two very fine poems familiar to readers of anthologies. He was not only a poet, but something of a philosopher, and entertained distinctly heretical views in religious matters. On the other hand, John Donne spoke well of him, and Ben Jonson was a friend and correspondent. For he enjoyed the society of men of letters, among whom he moved as an equal as well as among the courtiers of Europe and among ladies and gentlemen of fashion. In Edward the characteristic traits of the Herberts and some of the particular traits of Magdalen Herbert, his mother, appear to have been combined. In George, of frailer constitution and contemplative mind, we seem to find more of Magdalen; yet he was as proudly conscious of being a Herbert as any other Herbert, and at one period had the family inclination to life in the world of public affairs.

By far the most important for our study of George Herbert, of the men of letters and the scholars who delighted in the company of Magdalen Herbert, was John Donne. He was enough older in years to have the admiration of the younger man and to influence him: he was enough beneath Lady Herbert in rank to be almost a protégé. The friendship between Donne and Lady Herbert is commemorated in one of Donne's best known and most loved poems, 'The Autumnal', in which is found the couplet which every lover of Donne's poetry knows by heart:

> No Spring, nor Summer Beauty hath such grace
> As I have seen in one Autumnal face.

To the influence of Donne's poetry upon that of Herbert we shall return presently. Meanwhile it is in place to provide a brief survey of Herbert's life and a sketch of his character.

At the age of twelve George Herbert was sent to Westminster School, where he became proficient in the usual disciplines of Latin and Greek, and gained also— what is equally important for mention here—an advanced practice in music: not only in the choral singing for which that famous school was well known because of its association with the services in Westminster Abbey, but also with a difficult instrument—the lute. If we remember Herbert's knowledge of music, and his skill at the instrument, we appreciate all the better his mastery of lyric verse. From Westminster he went on to Trinity College Cambridge, being one of three boys of Westminster School who were given scholarships to that College at that time.

At Westminster School Herbert had an exemplary record. The relation of the school to the Abbey had also familiarised him with the church offices, in which the boys took part. (Their close attention to the sermon was ensured by the requirement that they should afterwards compose a summary of it in Latin.) At the university Herbert was equally forward; sober and staid in his conduct and diligent in his studies, he was given particular attention by the Master. It was said of him, however, that he was careful to be well, even expensively dressed; and that his attitude towards his fellow undergraduates of lower social position was distant, if not supercilious. Even Isaac Walton (his most nearly contemporary biographer) who tends to emphasise Herbert's saintliness, admits that Herbert, at this stage of his life, was very much aware of the consideration which he thought due to his exalted birth.

At the age of twenty-three Herbert was made a Fellow of his own college of Trinity. He began by instructing the younger undergraduates in Greek grammar; later he taught rhetoric and the rules of oratory. His health was never good; and the climate of Cambridge was somewhat harsh for a young man of frail constitution. His income as Fellow and Tutor was eked out by a small allowance from his brother Edward (the head of the family) and occasionally by gifts from his step-father. For his mother had, in middle age, married again, and was now the wife of Sir John Danvers. But Herbert's poor health meant doctors' bills and occasional absences from Cambridge; as a learned scholar of an active and curious mind he needed constantly to purchase books, and books were expensive, especially those which had to be imported from the continent. He therefore sought to improve his finances, and at the same time attain a position of considerable dignity, by obtaining appointment as Public Orator to the University.

Herbert had not yet formed the design of passing his life as a country parson. Indeed, the post of Public Orator was one which would bring him into the great world and even into contact with the court of James I. He achieved his aim; and during his tenure of this office acquired an extensive acquaintance, which his family connections and his own wide sympathies helped to enlarge. He greatly admired Sir Francis Bacon, a man of a type of mind very different from his own; another elder friend with whom he was on affectionate terms was the saintly Bishop Lancelot Andrewes. Nor did a wide divergence of religious attitude and belief diminish the warm regard between him and his elder brother Edward.

A Fellow of a College was expected to take holy orders in the Church of England within seven years of his appointment, or resign his Fellowship. Herbert was, like his mother, a practising and devout Anglican, but at this time his ambition looked toward the world of Court and Government. His violent attack, in the form of a Latin thesis, upon the Puritan position in the person of one of its most outrageous zealots, Andrew Melville, was his only sortie into religious controversy; though undoubtedly wholly sincere, Herbert probably aimed at winning the approval of King James. He would certainly have liked public office, but had neither the wiles of ingratiation, nor the means or the wish to buy his way in. His next step was to become Member of Parliament for Montgomery—an election which came to him almost as a matter of course as a member of the Herbert family. But this period of his life was not marked by success: two great noblemen of whose patronage he felt assured died, and the death of King James himself, in the following year, seems to have left him with little hope of a Secretaryship of State.

It was necessary to review this much of Herbert's early life to make the point that Herbert, though from childhood a pious member of the Anglican Church, and a vigorous opponent of the Puritans and Calvinists, felt no strong vocation to the priesthood until his thirty-first year. There were at least four persons in his life who may, by precept or example, have influenced him to this decision. His mother, to whom he was devotedly attached, was, we know, a woman not only of strong character, but of great piety. Two friends much older than himself have already been mentioned: Dr. John Donne and Bishop Andrewes. And finally, there was his dear friend Nicholas Ferrar of Little Gidding, an exemplar of High Churchmanship, whose domestic life approached that of a religious community. To Ferrar it was that he consigned, upon his death, the manuscript collection of verse upon which his fame is founded, the collection *The Temple* which we should not know had Ferrar not chosen to publish it; this he did in the same year in which Herbert died.[1]

---

[1] Four editions of *The Temple* appeared within three years of its first publication; its popularity continued to the end of the century. In the eighteenth century Herbert's poems were generally disparaged: Cowper, for instance, though he found in them a strain of piety which he admired, regarded them as 'gothick and uncouth', and this was the universal opinion of that age. The restoration of Herbert's reputation was begun by Coleridge who, in a letter to William Collins, dated 6 December 1818, writes: '. . . I find more substantial comfort now in pious George Herbert's 'Temple' which I used to read to amuse myself with his quaintness—in short, only to laugh at—than in all the poetry since the poems of Milton. If you have not read Herbert, I can recommend the book to you confidently. The poem entitled 'The Flower' is especially affecting; and, to me, such a phrase as 'and relish versing' expresses a sincerity, a reality, which I would unwillingly exchange for the more dignified 'and once more love the Muse' &c. And so, with many other of Herbert's homely phrases.' (Letters, vol. IV, edited by Earl Leslie Griggs, 1959.)

Writing to Lady Beaumont in 1826, Coleridge says: 'My dear old friend Charles Lamb and I differ widely (and in point of taste and moral feeling this is a rare occurrence) in our estimate and liking of George Herbert's sacred poems. He greatly prefers Quarles—nay he dislikes Herbert.' (The Letters of Charles Lamb, edited by E. V. Lucas, vol. I, 1935.)

Herbert's mother died in 1626. George Herbert was for a time a guest in the house of his step-father's elder brother, Lord Danvers, and in 1629, having already taken holy orders, he married Jane Danvers, the daughter of a cousin of Lord Danvers. It was a happy marriage. Six years after Herbert's death, his widow married Sir Robert Cook. In her widowhood, Isaac Walton says:

> . . . She continued mourning, till time and conversation had so moderated her sorrows, that she became the happy wife of Sir Robert Cook of Highnam in the County of Gloucester, Knight. And though he put a high value on the excellent accomplishments of her mind and body; and was so like Mr. Herbert, as not to govern like a Master, but as an affectionate Husband; yet she would even to him take occasion to mention the name of Mr. George Herbert, and say that name must live in her memory, till she put off mortality.

George Herbert died of consumption at the age of forty. For the last years of his life he had been Rector of the parish of Bemerton in Wiltshire. That he was an exemplary parish priest, strict in his own observances and a loving and generous shepherd of his flock, there is ample testimony. And we should bear in mind, that at the time when Herbert lived, it was most unusual that a man of George Herbert's social position should take orders and be content to devote himself to the spiritual and material needs of a small parish of humble folk in a rural village. From Walton's *Life* I must quote one anecdote:

> In another walk to *Salisbury*, he saw a poor man, with a poorer horse, that was fall'n under his Load; they were both in distress, and needed present help; which Mr. *Herbert* perceiving, put off his Canonical Coat, and help'd the poor man to unload, and after, to lead his horse: The poor man blest him for it: and he blest the poor man; and was so like the *good Samaritan* that he gave him money to refresh both himself and his horse; and told him, *That if he lov'd himself, he should be merciful to his Beast.* Thus he left the poor man, and at his coming to his musical friends at *Salisbury,*

they began to wonder that Mr. *George Herbert* which us'd to be so
trim and clean, came into the company so soyl'd and discompos'd;
but he told them the occasion: And when one of the company
told him, *He had disparag'd himself by so dirty an employment*; his
answer was, *That the thought of what he had done, would prove Musick
to him at Midnight; and that the omission of it would have upbraided
and made discord in his Conscience, whensoever he should pass by that
place; for, if I be bound to pray for all that be in distress, I am sure that
I am bound so far as it is in my power to practise what I pray for. And
though I do not wish for the like occasion every day, yet let me tell you,
I would not willingly pass one day of my life without comforting a sad
soul, or shewing mercy; and I praise God for this occasion:* And now
let's tune our instruments.

In this context is worth mention a prose treatise of
Herbert's entitled *A Priest to the Temple Or The Country
Parson His Character etc.* In this treatise he sets forth the duties
and responsibilities of the country parson to God, to his
flock, and to himself; and from what we know of Herbert
we can be sure that he practised, and always strove to
practise, what he here prescribes to other priests. The story
of the poor man and his horse is all the more touching when
we read that the Parson's apparell should be

> plaine, but reverend, and clean, without spots, or dust, or smell;
> the purity of his mind breaking out, and dilating it selfe even to
> his body, cloaths, and habitation.

We are told elsewhere in the same treatise that a priest who
serves as domestic chaplain to some great person is not to be

> over-submissive, and base, but to keep up with the Lord and Lady
> of the house, and to preserve a boldness with them and all, even so
> farre as reproofe to their very face, when occasion calls, but season-
> ably and discreetly.

The pride of birth natural to Herbert is transformed into

the dignity of the Servant of God. The parson, he continues, should be a man of wide reading: Herbert mentions the Church Fathers and the Scholastics, and tells us that the parson should be attentive to later writers also. The parson must give careful attention to his sermon, taking due account of the needs and capacities of his parishioners, and keeping their attention by persuading them that his sermon is addressed to this particular congregation and to one and all of them. And he should, especially when visiting the sick, or otherwise afflicted, persuade them to particular confession, 'labouring to make them understand the great good use of this antient and pious ordinance'.

We are not to presume, however, that George Herbert was naturally of a meek and mild disposition. He was, on the contrary, somewhat haughty; proud of his descent and social position; and, like others of his family, of a quick temper. In his poems we can find ample evidence of his spiritual struggles, of self-examination and self-criticism, and of the cost at which he acquired godliness.

> I struck the board, and cry'd, No more.
> I will abroad.
> What? shall I ever sigh and pine?
> My lines and life are free; free as the rode,
> Loose as the winde, as large as store.
> Shall I be still in suit?
> Have I no harvest but a thorn
> To let me bloud, and not restore
> What I have lost with cordiall fruit?
> Sure there was wine
> Before my sighs did drie it: there was corn
> Before my tears did drown it.
> Is the yeare onely lost to me?
> Have I no bayes to crown it?
> No flowers, no garlands gay? all blasted?
> All wasted?
> Not so, my heart: but there is fruit
> And thou hast hands.

Recover all they sigh-blown age
On double pleasures: leave thy cold dispute
Of what is fit and not. Forsake thy cage,
Thy rope of sands,
Which pettie thoughts have made, and made to thee
Good cable, to enforce and draw,
And be thy law,
Whilst thou didst wink and wouldst not see.
Away; take heed;
I will abroad.
Call in thy deaths head there: tie up thy fears.
He that forbears
To suit and serve his need
Deserves his load.
But as I rav'd and grew more fierce and wilde
At every word,
Me thoughts I heard one calling, *Child*!
And I reply'd, *My Lord.*

(*The Collar*)

To think of Herbert as the poet of a placid and comfortable
easy piety is to misunderstand utterly the man and his
poems. Yet such was the impression of Herbert and of the
Church of England given by the critic who wrote the
introduction to the World's Classics edition of Herbert's
Poems in 1907. For this writer, the Church of England, in
Herbert's day as well as in his own, is typified by a peaceful
country churchyard in the late afternoon:

> Here, as the cattle wind homeward in the evening light, the
> benign, white-haired parson stands at his gate to greet the cowherd,
> and the village chimes call the labourers to evensong. For these
> contented spirits, happily removed from the stress and din of
> contending creeds and clashing dogmas, the message of the gospel
> tells of divine approval for work well done. . . . And among these
> typical spirits, beacons of a quiet hope, no figure stands out more
> brightly or more memorably than that of George Herbert.

This rustic scene belongs to the world of Tennyson and
Dickens; but no more to the world of George Herbert than

to our world to-day. It is well that the latest World's Classics edition (the text based on that established by F. E. Hutchinson) has a new introduction by a learned and sensitive critic, Miss Helen Gardner. The earlier introduction gave a false picture both of Herbert and his poetry, and of the Church itself in an age of bitter religious conflict and passionate theology: it is worth quoting in order to point out how false a picture this is.

II

The poems on which George Herbert's reputation is based are those constituting the collection called *The Temple*. About *The Temple* there are two points to be made. The first is that we cannot date the poems exactly. Some of them may be the product of careful re-writing. We cannot take them as being necessarily in chronological order: they have another order, that in which Herbert wished them to be read. *The Temple* is, in fact, a structure, and one which may have been worked over and elaborated, perhaps at intervals of time, before it reached its final form. We cannot judge Herbert, or savour fully his genius and his art, by any selection to be found in an anthology; we must study *The Temple* as a whole.

To understand Shakespeare we must acquaint ourselves with all of his plays; to understand Herbert we must acquaint ourselves with all of *The Temple*. Herbert is, of course, a much slighter poet than Shakespeare; nevertheless he may justly be called a major poet. Yet even in anthologies he has for the most part been underrated. In Sir Arthur Quiller-Couch's *Oxford Book of English Verse*, which was for many years unchallenged in its representative character, George Herbert was allotted five pages—the same number as Bishop King and much less than Robert Herrick, the latter of whom, most critics of to-day would agree, is a poet of very much slighter gifts. For poetic range Herbert was commonly considered more limited than Donne; and for intensity he was compared unfavourably with Crashaw. This is the view even of Professor Grierson, to whom we are greatly indebted for his championship of Donne and those poets whose names are associated with that of Donne.

And here we must exercise caution in our interpretation of the phrase 'the school of Donne'. The present writer once contemplated writing a book under that title; and lately the title has been used by a distinguished younger critic for a study covering the same ground. The phrase is legitimate and useful to designate that generation of men younger than Donne whose work is obviously influenced by him, but we must not take it as implying that those poets who experienced his influence were for that reason lesser poets. (Professor Grierson, indeed, seems to consider Andrew Marvell the greatest, greater even than Donne.) That Herbert learned directly from Donne is self-evident. But to think of 'the school of Donne', otherwise 'the metaphysical poets', as Donne's inferiors, or to try to range them on a scale of greatness, would be to lose our way. What is important is to apprehend the particular virtue, the unique flavour of each one. Comparing them with any other group of poets at any other period, we observe the characteristics which they share: when we compare them with each other, their differences emerge clearly.

Let us compare a poem by Donne with a poem by Herbert; and as Herbert's poetry deals always with religious matter, we shall compare two religious sonnets. First, Donne:

> Batter my heart, three person'd God; for, you
> As yet but knocke, breathe, shine, and seeke to mend;
> That I may rise, and stand, o'erthrow mee', and bend
> Your force, to breake, blowe, burn and make me new.
> I, like an usurpt towne, to'another due,
> Labour to 'admit you, but Oh, to no end,
> Reason your viceroy in mee, mee should defend,
> But is captiv'd, and proves weake or untrue.

Yet dearely' I love you,' and would be loved faine,
But am betroth'd unto your enemie:
Divorce mee, 'untie, or break that knot againe;
Take mee to you, imprison mee, for I
Except you 'enthrall mee, never shall be free,
Nor ever chast, except you ravish mee.

And here is George Herbert:

Prayer (1)

Prayer the Churches banquet, Angels age,
  Gods breath in man returning to his birth,
  The soul in paraphrase, heart in pilgrimage,
The Christian plummet sounding heav'n and earth;
Engine against th' Almightie, sinners towre,
  Reversed thunder, Christ-side-piercing spear,
  The six-daies world transposing in an houre,
A kinde of tune, which all things heare and fear;
Softnesse, and peace, and joy, and love, and blisse,
  Exalted Manna, gladnesse of the best,
  Heaven in ordinarie, man well drest,
The milkie way, the bird of Paradise,
    Church-bels beyond the starres heard, the souls bloud,
    The land of spices; something understood.

The difference that I wish to emphasise is not that between the violence of Donne and the gentle imagery of Herbert, but rather a difference between the dominance of intellect over sensibility and the dominance of sensibility over intellect. Both men were highly intellectual, both men had very keen sensibility: but in Donne thought seems in control of feeling, and in Herbert feeling seems in control of thought. Both men were learned, both men were accustomed to preaching—but not to the same type of congregation. In Donne's religious verse, as in his sermons, there is much more of the *orator*: whereas Herbert, for all that he had been successful as Public Orator of Cambridge University, has a much more intimate tone of speech. We do not know what Herbert's sermons were like; but we can conjecture that

in addressing his little congregation of rustics, all of whom
he knew personally, and many of whom must have received
both spiritual and material comfort from him and from his
wife, he adopted a more homely style. Donne was accustomed to addressing large congregations (one is tempted to
call them 'audiences') out of doors at Paul's Cross, Herbert
only the local congregation of a village church.

The difference which I have in mind is indicated even by
the last two lines of each sonnet. Donne's

> ... for I
> Except you'enthrall me, never shall be free,
> Nor ever chast, unless you ravish mee

is, in the best sense, *wit*. Herbert's

> Church-bels beyond the starres heard, the souls bloud,
> The land of spices, something understood

is the kind of poetry which, like

> magic casements, opening on the foam
> Of perilous seas, in faery lands forlorn

may be called *magical*.

Of all the poets who may be said to belong to 'the school
of Donne', Herbert is the only one whose whole source of
inspiration was his religious faith. Most of the poetry upon
which rests the reputation of Donne is love poetry, and his
religious verse is of a later period in his life; his reputation,
and his influence upon other poets would have been as great
had he written no religious poetry at all. Richard Crashaw,
who had himself frequented the community of Nicholas
Ferrar at Little Gidding before his conversion to the Church
of Rome, might still have been a notable poet had he
written no religious verse—even though his devotional
poems are his finest. Herbert, before becoming Rector of
Bemerton, had never been a recluse: he had, in his short life,

wide acquaintance in the great world, and he enjoyed a happy marriage. Yet it was only in the Faith, in hunger and thirst after godliness, in his self-questioning and his religious meditation, that he was inspired as a poet. If there is another example since his time of a poetic genius so dedicated to God, it is that of Gerard Hopkins. We are certainly justified in presuming that no other subject-matter than that to which he confined himself could have elicited great poetry from George Herbert. Whether we regard this as a limitation, or as the sign of solitary greatness, of a unique contribution to English poetry, will depend upon our sensibility to the themes of which he writes.

It would, however, be a gross error to assume that Herbert's poems are of value only for Christians—or, still more narrowly, only for members of his own church. For the practising Christian, it is true, they may be aids to devotion. When I claim a place for Herbert among those poets whose work every lover of English poetry should read and every student of English poetry should study, irrespective of religious belief or unbelief, I am not thinking primarily of the exquisite craftmanship, the extraordinary metrical virtuosity, or the verbal felicities, but of the *content* of the poems which make up *The Temple*. These poems form a record of spiritual struggle which should touch the feeling, and enlarge the understanding of those readers also who hold no religious belief and find themselves unmoved by religious emotion. Professor L. C. Knights, in an essay on George Herbert in his *Explorations*, both expresses this doubt on the part of the non-Christian and dispels it:

> Even Dr. Hutchinson, whose superbly edited and annotated edition of the Complete Works is not likely to be superseded . . . remarks that 'if to-day there is a less general sympathy with Herbert's religion, the beauty and sincerity of its expression are appreciated by those who do not share it'. True, but there is much more than the 'expression' that we appreciate, as I shall try to show. Herbert's poetry is an integral part of the great English tradition.

Whether the religious poems of Donne show greater profundity of thought, and greater intensity of passion, is a question which every reader will answer according to his own feelings. My point here is that *The Temple* is not to be regarded simply as a collection of poems, but (as I have said,) as a record of the spiritual struggles of a man of intellectual power and emotional intensity who gave much toil to perfecting his verses. As such, it should be a document of interest to all those who are curious to understand their fellow men; and as such, I regard it as a more important document than all of Donne's *religious* poems taken together.

On the other hand, I find Herbert to be closer in spirit to Donne than is any other of 'the school of Donne'. As the personal bond, through Lady Herbert, was much closer, this seems only natural. Other powerful literary influences formed the manner of Crashaw, the Roman Catholic convert: the Italian poet Marino and the Spanish poet Gongora, and, we are told,[1] the Jesuit poets who wrote in Latin. Vaughan and Traherne were poets of mystical experience: each appears to have experienced early in life some mystical illumination which inspires his poetry. And the other important poet of the 'metaphysical' school, Andrew Marvell, is a master of secular and religious poetry equally. In my attempt to indicate the affinity of Herbert to Donne, and also the difference between them, I have spoken earlier of a 'balance' between the intellect and the sensibility. But equally well (for one has recourse to diverse and even mutually contradictory metaphors and images to express the inexpressible) we can speak of a 'fusion' of intellect and sensibility in different proportions. In the work of a later generation of 'metaphysicals'—notably Cleveland, Benlowes and Cowley—we encounter a kind of emotional drought, and a verbal ingenuity which, having no great depth of feeling to work upon, tends towards corruption of language,

---

[1] By Mario Praz, whose *Seicentismo e marinismo in Inghilterra* is essential for the study of Crashaw in particular.

and merits the censure which Samuel Johnson applies indiscriminately to all the 'school of Donne'.

To return to the import of *The Temple* for all perceptive readers whether they share Herbert's faith or no. Professor Knights quotes with approval Dr. Hutchinson's description of the poems as

> colloquies of the soul with God or self-communings which seek to bring order into that complex personality of his which he analyses so unsparingly,

but goes on to make a qualification which seems to me very important. Dr. Hutchinson believes that Herbert's principal temptation was *ambition*. We need not deny that Herbert had been, like many other men, ambitious; we know that he had a hot temper; we know that he liked fine clothes and fine company, and would have been pleased by preferment at Court. But beside the struggle to abandon thought of the attractions offered to worldly ambition, Professor Knights finds 'a dejection of spirit that tended to make him regard his own life, the life he was actually leading, as worthless and unprofitable'. Mr. Knights attributes the cause partly to ill-health, but still more to a *more ingrained distrust*. It was perhaps distrust of himself, or fear of testing his powers among more confident men, that drove him to the shelter of an obscure parsonage. He had, Mr. Knights suggests, to rid himself of the torturing sense of frustration and impotence and accept the validity of his own experience. If this is so, Herbert's weakness became the source of his greatest power, for the result was *The Temple*.

I have called upon Mr. Knights's testimony in evidence that Herbert is not a poet whose work is significant only for Christian readers; that *The Temple* is not to be taken as simply a devotional handbook of meditation for the faithful, but as the personal record of a man very conscious of weakness and failure, a man of intellect and sensibility who hungered and thirsted after righteousness. And that by its *content*, as well as because of its technical accomplishment, it is a work of importance for every lover of poetry. This is not, however, to suggest that it is unprofitable for us to study the text for closer understanding, to acquaint ourselves with the liturgy of the Church, with the traditional imagery of the Church, and identify the Biblical allusions. One long poem which has been subjected to close examination is 'The Sacrifice'. There are sixty-three stanzas of three lines each, sixty-one of which have the refrain 'Was ever grief like Mine?' I mention this poem, which is a very fine one, and not so familiar as are some of the shorter and more lyrical pieces, because it has been carefully studied by Professor William Empson in his *Seven Types of Ambiguity*, and by Miss Rosamund Tuve in her *A Reading of George Herbert*. The lines are to be taken as spoken by Christ upon the Cross. We need, of course, enough acquaintance with the New Testament to recognise references to the Passion. But we are also better prepared if we recognise the Lamentations of Jeremiah, and the Reproaches in the Mass of the Presanctified which is celebrated on Good Friday.

> *Celebrant:* I led thee forth out of Egypt, drowning Pharaoh in the Red Sea: and thou hast delivered me up unto the chief priests.
> *Deacon & Subdeacon:* O my people, what have I done unto thee, or wherein have I wearied thee? Testify against me.

It is interesting to note that Mr. Empson and Miss Tuve differ in their interpretation of the following stanza:

> *O all ye who passe by, behold and see;*
> Man stole the fruit, but I must climbe the tree;
> The tree of life to all, but onely me:
> > Was ever grief like mine?

Mr. Empson comments: 'He climbs the tree to repay what was stolen, as if he were putting the apple back'; and develops this explanation at some length. Upon this interpretation Miss Tuve observes rather tartly: 'All (Mr. Empson's) rabbits roll out of one small hat—the fact that

Herbert uses the time-honoured 'climb' for the ascent of the Cross, and uses the word 'must', to indicate a far deeper necessity than that which faces a small boy under a big tree.' Certainly, the image of *replacing* the apple which has been plucked is too ludicrous to be entertained for a moment. It is obvious that Christ 'climbs' or is 'lifted' up on the Cross in atonement for the sin of Adam and Eve; the verb 'climb' being used traditionally to indicate the *voluntary* nature of the sacrifice for the sins of the world. Herbert was, assuredly, familiar with the imagery used by the pre-Reformation Church. It is likely also that Donne, learned in the works of the scholastics, and also in the writings of such Roman theologians contemporary with himself as Cardinal Bellarmine, set a standard of scholarship which Herbert followed.

To cite such an instance as this, however, is not to suggest that the lover of poetry needs to prepare himself with theological and liturgical knowledge *before* approaching Herbert's poetry. That would be to put the cart before the horse. With the appreciation of Herbert's poems, as with all poetry, enjoyment is the beginning as well as the end. We must enjoy the poetry before we attempt to penetrate the poet's mind; we must enjoy it before we understand it, if the attempt to understand it is to be worth the trouble. We begin by enjoying poems, and lines in poems, which make an immediate impression; only gradually, as we familiarise ourselves with the whole work, do we appreciate *The Temple* as a coherent sequence of poems setting down the fluctuations of emotion between despair and bliss, between agitation and serenity, and the discipline of suffering which leads to peace of spirit.

The relation of enjoyment to belief—the question whether a poem has more to give us if we share the beliefs of its author, is one which has never been answered satisfactorily: the present writer has made some attempt to contribute to the solution of the problem, and remains dissatisfied with his attempts. But one thing is certain: that even if the reader enjoys a poem more fully when he shares the beliefs of the author, he will miss a great deal of possible enjoyment and of valuable experience if he does not seek the fullest understanding possible of poetry in reading which he must 'suspend his disbelief'. (The present writer is very thankful for having had the opportunity to study the *Bhagavad Gītā* and the religious and philosophical beliefs, so different from his own, with which the *Bhagavad Gītā* is informed.)

Some of the poems in *The Temple* express moods of anguish and sense of defeat or failure:

> At first thou gav'st me milk and sweetnesses;
> > I had my wish and way:
> My dayes were straw'd with flow'rs and happinesse;
> > There was no moneth but May.
> But with my yeares sorrow did twist and grow,
> And made a partie unawares for wo. . . .
>
> Yet, though thou troublest me, I must be meek;
> > In weaknesse must be stout.
> Well, I will change the service, and go seek
> > Some other master out.
> Ah my deare God! though I am clean forgot,
> Let me not love thee, if I love thee not.

The foregoing lines are from the first of five poems all of which bear the title 'Affliction'. In the first of two poems both of which are entitled 'The Temper', he speaks of his fluctuations of faith and feeling:

> How should I praise thee, Lord! how should my rymes
> > Gladly engrave thy love in steel,
> > If what my soul doth feel sometimes,
> > > My soul might ever feel!

The great danger, for the poet who would write religious verse, is that of setting down what he would like to feel rather than be faithful to the expression of what he really feels. Of such pious insincerity Herbert is never guilty. We need not look too narrowly for a steady progress in Herbert's religious life, in an attempt to discover a chronological order. He falls, and rises again. Also, he was accustomed to working over his poems; they may have circulated in manuscript among his intimates during his lifetime. What we can confidently believe is that every poem in the book is true to the poet's experience. In some poems there is a more joyous note, as in 'Whitsunday':

> Listen sweet Dove unto my song,
> And spread thy golden wings in me;
> Hatching my tender heart so long,
> Till it get wing, and flie away with thee. . . .

> Lord, though we change, thou art the same;
> The same sweet God of love and light:
> Restore this day, for thy great name,
> Unto his ancient and miraculous right.

In 'The Flower' we hear the note of serenity, almost of beatitude, and of thankfulness for God's blessings:

> How fresh, O Lord, how sweet and clean
> Are thy returns! ev'n as the flowers in spring;
> To which, besides their own demean,
> The late-past frosts tributes of pleasure bring.
> > Grief melts away
> > Like snow in May,
> As if there were no such cold thing.

> . . . . . .

> And now in age I bud again,
> After so many deaths I live and write;
> I once more smell the dew and rain,
> And relish versing: O my onely light,
> > It cannot be
> > That I am he
> On whom thy tempests fell all night.[1]

[1] A. Alvarez in *The School of Donne* says justly of this stanza: 'This is, I suppose, the most perfect and most vivid stanza in the whole of Herbert's work. But it is, in every sense, so natural that its originality is easily missed.' (See also Coleridge on this poem: footnote to p. 58.)

I cannot resist the thought that in this last stanza—itself a miracle of phrasing—the imagery, so apposite to express the achievement of faith which it records, is taken from the experience of the man of delicate physical health who had known much illness. It is on this note of joy in convalescence of the spirit in surrender to God, that the life of discipline of this haughty and irascible Herbert finds conclusion: *In His will is our peace*.

III

Of all the 'school of Donne' Herbert is the closest to the old Master. Two other fine poets of the group might just as well be said to belong to the 'school of Herbert'. The debt of Vaughan to Herbert can be shown by quotation; Herbert's most recent and authoritative editor, Dr. F. E. Hutchinson, says: 'there is no example in English literature of one poet adopting another poet's work so extensively.' As for Crashaw, he undoubtedly admired Herbert. Nevertheless, in spite of a continuity of influence and inspiration, we must remember that these four poets, who form a constellation of religious genius unparalleled in English poetry, are all highly individual, and very different from each other.

The resemblances and differences between Donne and Herbert are peculiarly fascinating. I have suggested earlier that the difference between the poetry of Donne and Herbert shows some parallel to the difference between their careers in the Church. Donne the Dean of St. Paul's, whose sermons drew crowds in the City of London; Herbert the shepherd of a little flock of rustics, to whom he laboured to explain the meaning of the rites of the Church, the significance of Holy Days, in language that they could understand. There are, however, lines which might have come from either, where we seem to hear the same voice—Herbert echoing the idiom or reflecting the imagery of Donne. There is at least one poem of Herbert's in which he plays with extended metaphor in the manner of Donne.

It is 'Obedience' where he uses legal terms almost throughout:

> My God, if writings may
> Convey a Lordship any way
> Whither the buyer and the seller please;
> Let it not thee displease,
> If this poore paper do as much as they.

. . . . .

> He that will passe his land,
> As I have mine, may set his hand
> And heart unto this Deed, when he hath read;
> And make the purchase spread
> To both our goods, if he to it will stand.

Such elaboration is not typical of Herbert. But there is *wit*
like that of Donne in 'The Quip'. One feels obliged to quote
the whole poem:

> The merrie world did on a day
> With his train-bands and mates agree
> To meet together, where I lay,
> And all in sport to geere at me.

> First, Beautie crept into a rose,
> Which when I pluckt not, Sir, said she,
> Tell me, I pray, Whose hands are those?
> *But thou shalt answer, Lord, for me.*

> Then Money came, and chinking still,
> What tune is this, poore man? said he:
> I heard in Musick you had skill.
> *But thou shalt answer, Lord, for me.*

> Then came brave Glorie puffing by
> In silks that whistled, who but he?
> He scarce allow'd me half an eie.
> *But thou shalt answer, Lord, for me.*

> Then came quick Wit and Conversation,
> And he would needs a comfort be,
> And, to be short, make an Oration.
> *But thou shalt answer, Lord, for me.*

> Yet when the houre of thy designe
> To answer these fine things shall come;
> Speak not at large; say, I am thine:
> And then they have their answer home.

Professor Knights observes very shrewdly: 'the personifications here have nothing in common with Spenser's allegorical figures or with the capitalised abstractions of the eighteenth century: "brave Glorie puffing by in silks that whistled" might have come straight from *The Pilgrim's Progress.*' How audible are these silks 'that whistled'! 'Puffing' is equally apt: the same participle is used, to produce another but equally striking effect, elsewhere:

> Sometimes Death, puffing at the doore,
> Blows all the dust about the floore.
>
> (*The Church Floore*)

Herbert is a master of the simple everyday word in the right place, and charges it with concentrated meaning, as in 'Redemption', one of the poems known to all readers of anthologies:

> Having been tenant long to a rich Lord,
>   Not thriving, I resolved to be bold,
>   And make a suit unto him, to afford
> A new small-rented lease, and cancell th'old.
> In heaven at his manour I him sought:
>   They told me there, that he was lately gone
>   About some land, which he had dearly bought
> Long since on earth, to take possession.
> I straight return'd, and knowing his great birth,
>   Sought him accordingly in great resorts;
>   In cities, theatres, gardens, parks, and courts:
> At length I heard a ragged noise and mirth
>   Of theeves and murderers: there I him espied,
>   Who straight, *Your suit is granted*, said, & died.

The phrase 'ragged noise and mirth' gives us, in four words, the picture of the scene to which Herbert wishes to introduce us.

There are many lines which remind us of Donne:

> What though my bodie runne to dust?
> Faith cleaves unto it, counting evr'y grain
> With an exact and most particular trust,
>   Reserving all for flesh again.
> <div align="right">(<i>Faith</i>)</div>

>   My God, what is a heart?
>   Silver, or gold, or precious stone,
>   Or starre, or rainbow, or a part
> Of all these things, or all of them in one?
> <div align="right">(<i>Mattens</i>)</div>

>   . . . learn here thy stemme
> And true descent; that when thou shalt grow fat,
>
> And wanton in thy cravings, thou mayst know,
> That flesh is but the glasse, which holds the dust
> That measures all our time; which also shall
> Be crumbled into dust. . . .
> <div align="right">(<i>Church-monuments</i>)</div>

> Lord, how can man preach thy eternall word?
>   He is a brittle crazie glasse: . . .
> <div align="right">(<i>The Windows</i>)</div>

>   My bent thoughts, like a brittle bow,
>   Did flie asunder: . . .
> <div align="right">(<i>Deniall</i>)</div>

Herbert must have learned from Donne the cunning use of
both the learned and the common word, to give the sudden
shock of surprise and delight.

> But man is close, reserv'd, and dark to thee:
>   When thou demandest but a heart,
>   He cavils instantly.
>   In his poore cabinet of bone
>   Sinnes have their box apart,
> Defrauding thee, who gavest two for one.
> <div align="right">(<i>Ungratefulnesse</i>)</div>

The fleet Astronomer can bore,
And thred the spheres with his quick-piercing minde:
He views their stations, walks from doore to doore,
Surveys, as if he had design'd
To make a purchase there: he sees their dances,
And knoweth long before
Both their full-ey'd aspects, and secret glances.
(*Vanitie*)

My thoughts are all a case of knives, . . .
(*Affliction IV.*)

The following lines are very reminiscent of Donne:

How soon doth man decay!
When clothes are taken from a chest of sweets
To swaddle infants, whose young breath
Scarce knows the way;
Those clouts are little winding sheets,
Which do consigne and send them unto death.
(*Mortification*)

Here and there one can believe that Herbert has unconsciously used a word, or a rhythm of Donne, in a very different context from that of the original, as perhaps in the first line of 'The Discharge':

Busie enquiring heart, what wouldst thou know?

Donne begins 'The Sunne Rising' with the line

Busie old foole, unruly Sunne. . .

If Herbert's line be an echo and not a mere coincidence—
the reader must form his own opinion—it is all the more
interesting because of the difference in subject matter between
the two poems. If Herbert, in writing a poem of religious
mortification, could echo a poem of Donne which is an
aubade of the lover's complaint that day should come so

soon, it suggests that the literary influence of the elder man upon the younger was profound indeed.

Herbert's metrical forms, however, are both original and varied. To have invented and perfected so many variations in the form of lyrical verse is evidence of native genius, hard work and a passion for perfection. Two of his poems are such as would be considered, if written by a poet to-day, merely elegant trifles: 'The Altar' and 'Easter Wings'. In each, there is a disposition of longer and shorter lines so printed that the poem has the shape, the one of an altar and the other of a pair of wings. Such a diversion, if employed frequently, would be tedious, distracting and trying to the eyesight and we must be glad that Herbert did not make further use of these devices: yet it is evidence of Herbert's care for workmanship, his restless exploration of variety, and of a kind of gaiety of spirit, a joy in composition which engages our delighted sympathy. The exquisite variations of form in the other poems of *The Temple* show a resourcefulness of invention which seems inexhaustible, and for which I know no parallel in English poetry. Here, we can only quote a stanza from each of a brief selection to suggest the astonishing variety:

> O my chief good,
> How shall I measure out thy bloud?
> How shall I count what thee befell,
>   And each grief tell?
>
>   (*Good Friday*)

> O blessed bodie! Whither are thou thrown?
> No lodging for thee, but a cold hard stone?
> So many hearts on earth, and yet not one
>   Receive thee?
>   (*Sepulchre*)

Poems in such measures as these, and more obviously 'The Sacrifice', which we have quoted earlier, seem to indicate an ear trained by the music of liturgy.

> Rise heart; thy Lord is risen. Sing his praise
>> Without delayes,
> Who takes thee by the hand, that thou likewise
>> With him mayst rise:
> That, as his death calcined thee to dust,
> His life may make thee gold, and much more, just.
>>>> (*Easter*)

The slow movement of the last line quoted above has something of the movement of the exquisite line which ends Donne's 'Nocturnall upon S. Lucies Day':

> Both the yeares, and the dayes deep midnight is.

Somewhat similar to the movement of 'Good Friday' (quoted above) is:

>>> Since, Lord, to thee
>> A narrow way and little gate
> Is all the passage, on my infancie
>>> Thou didst lay hold, and antedate
>>> My faith in me.
>>>> (*Holy Baptisme I*)

Close enough to the form of 'Holy Baptisme' for its difference to be all the more striking is:

> Lord, I confesse my sinne is great;
> Great is my sinne. Oh! gently treat
> With thy quick flow'r, thy momentarie bloom;
>>> Whose life still pressing
>>> Is one undressing,
> A steadie aiming at a tombe.
>>>> (*Repentance*)

The next quotation has a solemn liturgical movement suited to the subject-matter and the title:

> O Do not use me
> After my sinnes! look not on my desert,
> But on thy glorie! then thou wilt reform
> And not refuse me: for thou onely art
> The mightie God, but I a sillie worm;
> O do not bruise me!
>
> (*Sighs and Grones*)

Herbert knows the effect of denying a rhyme where it is expected:

> When my devotions could not pierce
> Thy silent eares;
> Then was my heart broken, as was my verse:
> My breast was full of fears
> And disorder:
> (*Deniall*)

The roughness of metre of the line

> Then was my heart broken, as was my verse

is exactly what is wanted to convey the meaning of the words. The following stanza has an apparent artlessness and conversational informality which only a great artist could achieve:

> Lord, let the Angels praise thy name.
> Man is a foolish thing, a foolish thing,
> Folly and Sinne play all his game.
> His house still burns, and yet he still doth sing,
> *Man is but grasse,*
> *He knows it, fill the glasse.*
>
> (*Miserie*)

The next poem to be quoted is one of several poems of Herbert which, while being, like all the rest of his work, personal, have been set to music and sung as hymns:

> King of Glorie, King of Peace,
> I will love thee:
> And that love may never cease,
> I will move thee.
>
> (*Praise II*)

The same masterly simplicity is visible in:

> Throw away thy rod,
> Throw away thy wrath:
>   O my God,
> Take the gentle path.
>
>   (*Discipline*)

I wish to end by giving in full the poem which, significantly, I think, ends *The Temple*. It is named 'Love III', and indicates the serenity finally attained by this proud and humble man:

> Love bade me welcome: yet my soul drew back,
>   Guiltie of dust and sinne.
> But quick-ey'd Love, observing me grow slack
>   From my first entrance in,
> Drew nearer to me, sweetly questioning,
>   If I lack'd any thing.
>
> A guest, I answer'd, worthy to be here:
>   Love said, You shall be he.
> I the unkinde, ungratefull? Ah my deare,
>   I cannot look on thee.
> Love took my hand, and smiling did reply,
>   Who made the eyes but I?
>
> Truth Lord, but I have marr'd them: let my shame
>   Go where it doth deserve.
> And know you not, sayes Love, who bore the blame?
>   My deare, then I will serve.
> You must sit down, sayes Love, and taste my meat:
>   So I did sit and eat.

GEORGE HERBERT

Select Bibliography

BIBLIOGRAPHIES

PALMER, GEORGE HERBERT. *A Herbert Bibliography*. Cambridge: Privately Printed, 1911.
A catalogue of the compiler's collection of books by and about Herbert. Useful but incomplete.

TANNENBAUM, SAMUEL A. and DOROTHY R. *George Herbert: A Concise Bibliography*. Elizabethan Bibliographies No. 35. New York: Samuel A. Tannenbaum, 1946.

HUTCHINSON, FRANCIS E., ed. *The Works*. Oxford: Clarendon Press, 1941; corrected reprints, 1945, 1953.
Contains a bibliography.

CONCORDANCE

MANN, CAMERON. *A Concordance to the English Poems of George Herbert*. Boston and New York: Houghton Mifflin, 1927.

SOME COLLECTED EDITIONS

The Works. With a Preface by W. Pickering and Notes by S. T. Coleridge. 2 vols. London: Pickering, 1836.

The Complete Works. Edited by Alexander B. Grosart. Fuller Worthies' Library. 3 vols. London: Privately Printed, 1874.

The English Works Newly Arranged. Edited by George Herbert Palmer. 3 vols. Boston and New York: Houghton Mifflin, 1905.
An important edition, notwithstanding some editorial liberties and speculations.

The Works. Edited by Francis E. Hutchinson (see above).
The standard edition.

The Poems. Introduction by Helen Gardner. 2nd ed. The World's Classics. New York: Oxford University Press, 1961.

SEPARATE WORKS

Dates of original editions are given, and some modern editions are also recorded here.

The Temple, Sacred Poems and Private Ejaculations. Cambridge, 1633.
Thirteen editions were published before 1709 but none thereafter till 1799. The edition edited by Francis Meynell, with a bibliographical note by Geoffrey Keynes (London: Nonesuch Press, 1927) is based on the Bodleian MS which was the copy licensed in 1633 for the printer by the Cambridge Vice-Chancellor and his assessors.

Outlandish Proverbs Selected by Mr. G. H. London, 1640.
Enlarged as *Jacula Prudentum* (London, 1651).

Herbert's Remains. London, 1652.
Contains most of *A Priest to the Temple,* and *Jacula Prudentum.*

A Priest to the Temple, or, The Country Parson, His Character, and Rule of Holy Life. 1671.
Selected and edited by G. M. Forbes (London: Faith, 1949).

Herbert contributed Latin and Greek poems to a number of memorial collections, including *Lacrymae Cantabrigienses, in Obitum Reginae Annae* (Cambridge, 1619); *Memoriae Francisci, Baronis de Verulamio, Sacrum* (London, 1626); and *A Sermon of Commemoration of the Lady Danvers by John Donne. Together with other Commemorations of her, by her Son, G. Herbert* (London, 1627).

Further details in the edition of *The Works* by Francis E. Hutchinson (see above).

RECORDING

Selections from The Temple. Ann Arbor: Idiom Recording Co. El LKC 3277. Read by Austin Warren.

BIOGRAPHICAL AND CRITICAL STUDIES OF HERBERT

The Life of Edward, Lord Herbert of Cherbury. Strawberry-Hill, 1764.
Edited by Sidney Lee (London: Nimmo, 1886).
See also *The Poems, English and Latin, of Edward Lord Herbert.* Edited by G. C. Moore Smith (Oxford: Clarendon Press, 1928).

TUVE, ROSEMOND. *A Reading of George Herbert.* Chicago: University of Chicago Press, 1952.
An important book.

BOTTRALL, MARGARET. *George Herbert.* London: John Murray, 1954.

SUMMERS, JOSEPH H. *George Herbert*. Cambridge: Harvard University Press, 1954.

CHUTE, MARCHETTE. *Two Gentle Men*. New York: Dutton, 1959. Biographies of Herbert and Herrick.

RICHARD CRASHAW

by Margaret Willy

Richard Crashaw was born in London in 1612. He died on 21 August 1649, in Italy.

RICHARD CRASHAW

Poet and *Saint*! to thee alone are given
The two most sacred *Names* of *Earth* and *Heaven*.

THUS, seven years after his friend's death, Cowley apostrophized Richard Crashaw. A writer in 1657 named Crashaw in the same breath as the 'refined witts' of Bacon, Sidney, Ben Jonson, Donne, and Shakespeare; and thirty years later another critic was acclaiming him as 'the Darling of the Muses . . . charming the ear with a holy Rapture'. During the next hundred years Crashaw's reputation suffered the inevitable decline. But the nineteenth century found Coleridge declaring: 'Where he does combine richness of thought and diction nothing can excel.' Lines 43–64 of Crashaw's *A Hymn to the Name and Honor of the Admirable Sainte Teresa* had, he added, been constantly with him while he was writing the second part of *Christabel:* 'if indeed, by some subtle process of the mind they did not suggest the first thought of the whole poem.' Today Crashaw has less general appeal than Donne and Herbert; although Mr T. S. Eliot finds him 'sometimes more profound and less sectarian' than either Herbert or Vaughan.

Born in London in 1612, the poet was the only son of a then famous father, the Puritan preacher and controversialist, William Crashaw. He was educated at the Charterhouse School, where he had a thorough grounding in the classical poets and in writing verse exercises in imitation of their style. To this, no doubt, he owed something of the ability attributed to him in the Preface to his *Steps to the Temple*: of having, 'under locke and key in readinesse, the richest treasures of the best Greeke and Latine Poets, some of which Authors hee had . . . at his command by heart'.

In 1631 Crashaw went up to Pembroke College, Cambridge, and three years later took his degree; also, in the same year, publishing a volume of Latin epigrams on selected New Testament texts entitled *Epigrammatum Sacrorum Liber*. In 1635 he became a Fellow of Peterhouse, then the centre of Laudian High Churchmanship in Cambridge. For eight years Crashaw enjoyed the 'little contentfull kingdom', as he called it, of his 'beloved Patrimony in St. Peter'. Although the date of his ordination is not known, he served, during this time, as curate in the adjoining church of Little St. Mary's. His earliest biographer refers in glowing terms to the eloquence of Crashaw's preaching there ('those thronged Sermons on each Sunday and Holiday, that ravished more like Poems . . . scattering not so much Sentences as Extasies'). None of these, unfortunately, has survived.

It was in his Cambridge years, too, that Crashaw became friendly with Nicholas Ferrar, founder of the Anglican community at Little Gidding, and was a frequent visitor at the celebrated vigils there.

Like all his friends and colleagues, he was a staunch Royalist; and two years after the outbreak of civil war he was ejected from his Fellowship by the Parliamentary Commissioners. Thenceforth Crashaw's biography is a history of rootlessness, frustration, and repeated disappointments. He was for a time in Holland, and later in Paris; where, about 1646—according to the contemporary historian Anthony à Wood—Cowley found him, 'being a meer Scholar and very shiftless . . . in a sorry condition'. Crashaw had by now become converted to the Roman Catholic faith; and Henrietta Maria, exiled in Paris, addressed a dispatch to the Pope recommending the poet and his edifying example (praise echoed by Cowley in his elegy:

> His *Faith* perhaps in some nice Tenents might
> Be wrong; his *Life*, I'm sure, was *in the right*.)

The Queen's influence had little effect. Although Crashaw

went at once to Rome, he was still there, waiting, over a year later, suffering from poverty and ill-health. He obtained, for a time, some employment in the service of Cardinal Palotto. But by 1649, shortly after his appointment to a post at the Cathedral of Loreto, Crashaw was dead (according to Cowley, of a fever) at the early age of thirty-seven.

Steps to the Temple. Sacred Poems, with other Delights of the Muses, had been published in London in 1646, followed by a new edition including a number of fresh pieces in 1648. With its substantial recasting of poems from the earlier volume, this second edition offers interesting evidence of Crashaw's habit of polishing, revising, and amplifying his work: often pruning stylistic extravagances (as, for example, some of the alterations made in the final versions of *The Weeper* and *A Hymne of the Nativity*) in favour of more concrete expression. The additional poems show, too, that three wretched years of exile nevertheless yielded a good deal of creative activity. To the time between 1648 and Crashaw's death belong the 'divine' poems which came out for the first time in 1652 in *Carmen Deo Nostro*, published posthumously in Paris. This book, however, consisted largely of poems which had appeared in their revised versions in 1648 or were first printed there.

The anonymous writer of the Preface to *Steps to the Temple* (possibly Crashaw's friend and fellow-poet Joseph Beaumont, a Peterhouse colleague who after the Restoration became Master of the College) speaks of Crashaw as being 'excellent in five Languages . . . *vid*. Hebrew, Greek, Latine, Italian, Spanish, the two last whereof hee had little helpe in, they were of his owne acquisition'. Crashaw's reading in other languages played an important part in the development of his work. As already mentioned, he had been trained as a schoolboy in the artificial rhetoric of the Latin and Greek epigram; and as an undergraduate, much influenced by the style and spirit of Ovid, he continued these exercises. Many of Crashaw's essays in religious epigram show his gift for the striking phrase and achieve a concentrated intensity of poetic impact. This mastery of epigram reveals itself in his longer poems in the single telling line: as in 'Immortall Hony for the Hive of Loves' (*Sospetto d'Herode*); 'Candidates of blissefull Light' (*To the Name of Jesus*); or in the final line of his poem on the Circumcision, 'This knife may be the speares *Praeludium*'.

Still more potent in his evolution as a poet was Crashaw's self-acquired knowledge of Spanish and Italian. The life and work of St. Teresa of Avila, canonized in 1622, made a deep impression on his imagination. As he wrote of her:

> What soule soever in any Language can
> Speake heaven like hers, is my soules country-man.

Equally pervasive was the influence of the Neapolitan poet Marino. In Marino's relentless emphasis on literal detail and in the highly-coloured, flamboyant elements in his style, Crashaw found encouragement for a strain of sensationalism in his own temperament. To this Italian influence we owe much of Crashaw's habit of elaborating, for their own sake, merely decorative metaphors which neither advance the movement nor illuminate the inward truth of a poem. Some of his poetic lapses into banality and bad taste, exhibiting the worst excesses of the 'metaphysical conceit' (see *The Weeper*), as well as his exercise of wit in arid surface ingenuities, derived largely from Marino.

The cult of the emblem, then so popular in England and on the Continent, also made a distinct contribution to the shaping of Crashaw's style. Originating in medieval fable and allegory, emblems were allusive, often highly ingenious drawings symbolizing some moral precept, with companion verses translating the picture into words. With that of the *impresa* or heroic symbol, which epitomized a character or life by means of a single abstract sign, the influence of the emblem is plain in Crashaw's pictorial representation of abstract ideas and in his constant blend of literal with figurative, of homely realistic image with symbolic sublime.

Crashaw's happiness in his 'little contentfull kingdom' of Peterhouse shows that his was a nature well satisfied by a life of study and contemplation. The 'soft silken Houres' envisaged with:

> That not impossible shee
> That shall command my heart and mee;

in *Wishes to his supposed Mistresse*, never in fact became reality. Perhaps Crashaw's truer desire was expressed in his epigram *On Marriage*:

> I would be married, but I'de have no Wife,
> I would be married to a single Life.

A college fellowship then imposed upon its holder the rule of celibacy; so when, some time about 1645, Crashaw entered the Roman Catholic Church, he merely exchanged one mode of monastic existence for another. Admiring the Lessian virtues of temperance and abstinence,[1] he had consciously chosen the contemplative way. Thomas Car says of him in his introductory verses to *Carmen Deo Nostro*:

> No care
> Had he of earthly trashe. What might suffice
> To fitt his soule to heavenly exercise,
> Sufficed him. . . .
> What he might eate or weare he tooke no thought.
> His needful foode he rather found than sought.

And yet, as Joan Bennett points out in *Four Metaphysical Poets*: 'The images of the ascetic Crashaw are far more predominantly sexual than those of Donne, who had known the pleasures of sensuality, or of Herbert, who never seems to have desired them.' The needs of an enthusiastic and warmly emotional nature, disciplined by asceticism, found liberation both in the ritual of the Church whose shelter

---

[1] Crashaw's commendatory poem *In praise of Lessius his rule of Health* had accompanied the 1634 Cambridge translation of Lessius' *Hygiasticon*.

Crashaw finally sought, and in poetic expression of his religious experience and belief; sometimes, in his poetry, betraying him into extravagance, a lush and cloying oversweetness. For him the sensuous is present in, and inextricable from, his conception of the most rarefied spiritual experience. The exalted mystical communion of the soul with God—of

> the divine embraces
> Of the deare spowse of spirits—

is communicated in terms of languorous physical sensation:

> Amorous Languishments, Luminous trances,
>   Sights which are not seen with eyes,
> Spirituall and soule peircing glances.
>   Whose pure and subtle lightning, flies
> Home to the heart, and setts the house on fire;
> And melts it downe in sweet desire. . . .

> . . . Delicious deaths, soft exhalations
> Of soule; deare, and divine annihilations.
>   A thousand unknowne rites
>   Of joyes, and rarifyed delights.

> (*On a prayer booke sent to Mrs. M. R.*)

The poet goes on to invoke the joys of Divine love, the experience of the soul who:

> . . . shall discover,
>   What joy, what blisse,
> How many heavens at once it is,
> To have a God become her lover,

in symbols of the 'pure inebriating pleasures' known to human sense.

Constantly Crashaw uses images of physical love—of 'birth, milk and all the rest', as Gerard Manley Hopkins put it in a poem peculiarly reminiscent of Crashaw—to communicate his perceptions of its spiritual and divine counterpart.

Mary Magdalene's eyes are 'swolne wombes of sorrow'; the Easter sepulchre is 'Natures new wombe, . . . faire Immortalities perfumed Nest'; while the day of Christ's name coming to earth is welcomed as the 'Womb of Day' and exhorted to:

> Unfold thy fair Conceptions; And display
> The Birth of our Bright Joyes.

There are, too, the many 'nursing' images: 'Two sister-Seas of Virgins Milke' in *A Hymne of the Nativity;* the infant martyrs' heaven, which will be 'at the worst/Milke all the way'; or in *The Weeper,* where heaven's bosom drinks the 'gentle stream' of the Magdalene's tears:

> Where th' milky rivers creep
> Thine floates above; and is the cream.

The nest, both as refuge sheltered by parental protection and the nourishing source of all love, is one of the most frequently recurring symbols in Crashaw's work.

From the same, sensuous source in his nature sprang Crashaw's characteristic, often, it must seem to us, morbid, preoccupation with experiences of physical agony in a religious context. His detailed, intensely literal attention to different aspects of Christ's body (as in the poem on the Circumcision and those on the Passion) owes much, of course, to Marino, and something to a European form of contemplative exercise which influenced other English religious verse of the time. Some of Crashaw's epigrams and lyrics on these subjects actually originate in lines by the Italian poet. Nevertheless, an obsessive compulsion to contemplate, even luxuriate in, bodily torment does seem to be an undoubted trait of Crashaw's poetic individuality. He speaks of Christ's torturers clothing Him in the rich garment of His own blood, 'Opening the purple wardrobe of thy side', and declares that 'Not a haire but payes his River/ To this *Red Sea* of thy blood'. In writing of the Christian martyrs Crashaw elaborates, almost voluptuously, the visual aspect of their sufferings. The weapons of their persecutors, he says:

> sett wide the Doores
> For Thee: Fair, purple Doores, of love's devising;
> The Ruby windows which inrich't the EAST
> Of Thy so oft repeated Rising.
> Each wound of Theirs was Thy new Morning;
> And reinthron'd thee in thy Rosy Nest . . .

The poem *On the wounds of our crucified Lord*, with its conjunction of bleeding flesh with erotic imagery, implicitly identifies and fuses the anguish of crucifixion with sensations of love:

> O these wakefull wounds of thine!
>   Are they Mouthes? or are they eyes?
> Be they Mouthes, or be they eyne,
>   Each bleeding part some one supplies.
>
> Lo! a mouth, whose full-bloom'd lips
>   At too deare a rate are roses.
> Lo! a blood-shot eye! that weepes
>   And many a cruell teare discloses . . .
>
> This foot hath got a Mouth and lippes,
>   To pay the sweet summe of thy kisses . . .

Clearly the wounds of martyrdom symbolized for Crashaw the most complete and eloquent physical expression of spiritual love. As he says in one of his poems to St. Teresa:

> For in love's field was never found
> A nobler weapon than a WOUND.

Crashaw wrote three poems celebrating the life of this saint, and her martyrdom.[1] The first of them (that praised

[1] In fact St. Teresa died a natural death.

by Coleridge), *A Hymn to the Name and Honor of the Admirable Sainte Teresa*, with its superb opening lines:

> Love, thou art Absolute sole lord
> OF LIFE and DEATH,

is among Crashaw's finest and most fully realized poems. Here again we hear the note of pleasure in pain:

> O how oft shalt thou complain
> Of a sweet and subtle PAIN.
> Of intolerable JOYES;
> Of a DEATH, in which who dyes
> Loves his death, and dyes again.
> And would for ever so be slain.

It should, however, be noted that the same idea, of an extremity of physical pain mounting to merge in spiritual bliss, occurs in the autobiographical *La Vida de la Santa Madre Teresa de Jesus*, an English translation of which appeared in 1642 and with which Crashaw was doubtless familiar.

The concluding invocation of his third St. Teresa poem, *The Flaming Heart upon the Book and Picture of the Seraphicall Saint Teresa*, rises to a height of lyrical rapture unsurpassed anywhere in Crashaw's work:

> O thou undaunted daughter of desires!
> By all thy dow'r of LIGHTS & FIRES;
> By all the eagle in thee, all the dove;
> By all thy lives & deaths of love;
> By thy large draughts of intellectuall day,
> And by thy thirsts of love more large than they;
> By all thy brim-fill'd Bowles of fierce desire
> By thy last Morning's draught of liquid fire;
> By the full kingdome of that finall kisse
> That seiz'd thy parting Soul, & seal'd thee his;
> By all the heav'ns thou hast in him
> (Fair sister of the SERAPHIM)
> By all of HIM we have in THEE;
> Leave nothing of my SELF in me.
> Let me so read thy life, that I
> Unto all life of mine may dy.

Just as Crashaw seems to savour the pleasurable sensations of pain, he likewise invites and finds a similar sweetness in grief:

> Welcome my Griefe, my Joy; how deare's
> To me my Legacy of Teares!

or, in *The Weeper*:

> No where but here did ever meet
> Sweetnesse so sad, sadnesse so sweet.

Even allowing for the special fascination tears held for the seventeenth-century metaphysical poet (see, among other poems, Donne's *A Valediction: of weeping*, Marvell's *Eyes and Tears*, and Thomas Vaughan's *The Stone*), their attraction for Crashaw appears peculiarly compelling. The very thought of them at once conjures for him a multitude of affinities, with stars, diamonds, pearls, watery blossoms, liquid jewels and rain-showers, streams and milky rivers, seas and floods. He writes an epigram on the tears of Lazarus, exhorts them from Pilate, and devotes a well-known poem, *The Teare*, to those of the Virgin; while in his lines *Upon the Death of a Gentleman* he declares:

> Eyes are vocall, Teares have Tongues,
> And there be words not made with lungs;
> Sententious showers, ô let them fall,
> Their cadence is Rhetoricall.

Tears are the central, sustaining image of *The Weeper:* a poem strongly influenced by Marino in subject, stanza form, and even specific phrases, although the intensity of religious emotion and of vision are Crashaw's own. Here the object of contemplation, and starting-point for elaborating the various ideas they suggest to him, are the weeping eyes of Mary Magdalene ('sister springs! Parents of sylver-footed rills'). The timelessness of her ever-falling tears, as well as the dignity and majesty of sorrow, are finely communicated in stanzas 23 ('Does the day-starre rise?') and 26 ('Not, so long she lived'). Among the exuberant fancies Crashaw's imagination calls up are that of a 'brisk Cherub' sipping the Magdalene's tears, so that 'his song/Tasts of this Breakfast all day long'; and of a heavenly feast (with verbal echoes of Donne's *Twicknam Garden*) at which:

> Angels with crystall violls come
> And draw from these full eyes of thine
> Their master's Water: their own Wine.

But the lines most frequently quoted, in illustration of how precipitately the metaphysical conceit could plunge a poet into bathos, are Crashaw's description of Christ being:

> follow'd by two faithfull fountaines;
> Two walking baths; two weeping motions;
> Portable, & compendious oceans.

To the modern mind the whole visual suggestion is keenly ludicrous. Yet (as L. C. Martin points out in the Commentary to his edition of Crashaw's poems) what seems to us the incongruity of mundane epithets like 'portable' and 'compendious' in such a context, and of the prosaically concrete 'bath' metaphor, has in fact many parallels in both English and Continental poetry of the time.

That element in his nature which sometimes led Crashaw into poetic excess was also the source of his greatest strength. The strong sensuous vein lends his work a special purity, warmth and sweetness; a limpid flow of cadence whose music appeals to the ear as powerfully as its impressions of scent, light and colour entrance the other senses. Crashaw writes best when apparently with most ease and simplicity, his utterance unclogged by lush imagery or artificial conceits. This can be seen in the extracts from his St. Teresa poems quoted above; in the melodious tenderness of the shepherds' *Hymne of the Nativity*, full of such felicities as 'Love's architecture is his own'; in the second stanza of *Easter Day*:

> Of all the Gloryes Make Noone gay
>   This is the Morne.
> This rocke buds forth the fountaine of the streames
>   of Day.
>
>   In joyes white Annals live this houre,
>   When life was borne,
>   No cloud scoule on his radiant lids no tempest lowre,

or these from *Sospetto d'Herode*:

> That the Great Angell-blinding light should shrinke
> His blaze, to shine in a poore Shepheards eye.
> That the unmeasur'd God so low should sinke,
> As Pris'ner in a few poore Rags to lye . . .
> . . . That a vile Manger his low Bed should prove,
>   Who in a Throne of stars Thunders above.
>
> That hee whom the Sun serves, should faintly peepe
> Through clouds of Infant flesh: that hee the old
> Eternall Word should bee a Child, and weepe.
> That hee who made the fire, should feare the cold . . .

This poem, Crashaw's translation of the first canto of Marino's *La Strage degli Innocenti*, is far more striking in concreteness of imagery and atmospheric detail than its original. Here especially—in the mellifluous cadences, crowding personifications, and above all in the use of sensuous richness to communicate moral sentiment and spiritual meaning—Crashaw's debt to Spenser is plain. The pictorial and musical qualities of his verse may have owed something also to his natural talents for 'Musicke, Drawing, Limning, Graving' mentioned in the Preface to *Steps to the Temple*. (It is thought that at least two engravings in *Carmen Deo Nostro* were his own illustrations.) With his fragrant showers dropping 'a delicious dew of spices', his perfumed and balmy air, his lambs in the 'laughing meads' and sun-gilded fleece of grazing flocks, his April flowers and 'pure streames of the springing day', Crashaw at his best has the vernal freshness, delicacy, and radiance of Botticelli.

RICHARD CRASHAW

Select Bibliography

BIBLIOGRAPHIES
MARTIN, LEONARD C., ed. *The Poems, English, Latin, and Greek*. 2nd ed. Oxford: Clarendon Press, 1957.
Contains a bibliography.

WALLERSTEIN, RUTH C. *Richard Crashaw: A Study in Style and Poetic Development*. University of Wisconsin Studies in Language and Literature No. 37. Madison: University of Wisconsin, 1935; reprinted, 1959.
Contains a full bibliography.

SOME COLLECTED EDITIONS
The Complete Works. Edited by Alexander B. Grosart. Fuller Worthies' Library. 2 vols. London: Privately Printed, 1872–1873.

The Poems, English, Latin, and Greek. 2nd ed. Edited by Leonard C. Martin (see above).
The standard edition, with a bibliography and a biography. Contains additions and corrections to the first edition, 1927.

The Verse in English. New York: Grove Press, 1949.

SEPARATE WORKS
Dates of original editions are given.

Epigrammatum Sacrorum Liber. Cambridge, 1634.

Steps to the Temple. London, 1646; 2nd ed., with additions, 1648.
Edited by Alfred R. Waller (Cambridge: University Press, 1904).

Carmen Deo Nostro, Te Decet Hymnus, Sacred Poems. Paris, 1652.

A Letter from Mr. Crashaw to the Countess of Denbigh. London, 1653(?).

Poemata et Epigrammata. 2nd ed. Cambridge, 1670.

BIOGRAPHICAL AND CRITICAL STUDIES OF CRASHAW
WALLERSTEIN, RUTH C. *Richard Crashaw: A Study in Style and Poetic Development* (see above).

WARREN, AUSTIN. *Richard Crashaw: A Study in Baroque Sensibility*. Baton Rouge: Louisiana State University Press, 1939; Ann Arbor: University of Michigan Press, 1957.

PRAZ, MARIO. *Richard Crashaw*. Brescia: Morcelliana, 1946.

WILLEY, BASIL. *Richard Crashaw*. Cambridge: University Press, 1949.
A perceptive and illuminating memorial lecture delivered at Peterhouse, Cambridge (where Crashaw held a Fellowship), to mark the three-hundredth anniversary of the poet's death.

RICKEY, MARY E. *Rhyme and Meaning in Richard Crashaw*. Lexington: University of Kentucky Press, 1961.

WILLIAMS, GEORGE W. *Image and Symbol in the Sacred Poetry of Richard Crashaw*. Columbia: University of South Carolina Press, 1963.

HENRY VAUGHAN

by Margaret Willy

Henry Vaughan was born in 1621 or early in 1622 at Newton St. Bridget, Brecknockshire. He died in Wales on 23 April 1695.

HENRY VAUGHAN

Perhaps through Nicholas Ferrar at Little Gidding, Crashaw knew, and much admired, the work of George Herbert. He sent to a friend, as an aid to prayer, a copy of Herbert's poems, and probably derived from Herbert's *The Temple* the title for his own first volume; while the writer of the Preface to *Steps to the Temple* declared that 'Here's Herbert's second, but equall, who hath retriv'd Poetry of late'.

In Henry Vaughan, Herbert found a still more devout disciple. Vaughan's Preface to *Silex Scintillans* refers to 'the blessed man, *Mr. George Herbert*, whose holy *life* and *verse* gained many pious *Converts*, (of whom I am the least)'. In all his work after the first volume the influence of Herbert is pervasive, not only in subject and spirit, but in many obvious echoes of Herbert's titles, metres, and phrases.[1] That Vaughan was, however, no mere imitator of the man who was his acknowledged master in both his poetry and his religious life, can be seen in the finest poems in *Silex Scintillans*. In this volume Herbert's influence, though nowhere stronger, has been assimilated and transmuted by Vaughan's individual way of seeing. At his best he speaks with the distinctive voice of a poet in his own right: one whose apprehension of reality is different from Herbert's (especially in their respective attitudes to nature); who is more lyrical in the soaring of his religious exaltation or grief; and who, at his moments of intensest spiritual

---

[1] These are far too numerous to cite here. Readers interested in tracing the similarities and borrowings should see the Notes to L. C. Martin: *The Works of Henry Vaughan* (second edition, 1957), especially those to *Silex Scintillans*, pp. 727–751.

vision, 'sees *Invisibles*' with a quality of mystical rapture quite outside Herbert's scope.

Henry Vaughan and his younger twin, Thomas, were born in 1621 or early in 1622 at Newton St. Bridget, Brecknockshire, by the River Usk. Vaughan spent most of his life in Wales; and on all his books after the first he called himself by the title 'Silurist', after the ancient tribe of Silures which had once inhabited that south-eastern district of his native country. The boys were educated locally by Matthew Herbert, rector of a neighbouring parish. In 1638 they went up to Jesus College, Oxford; Henry being, he says, 'designed by my father for the study of the Law'.

Like that of Crashaw, though neither so permanently nor disastrously, Vaughan's career suffered through the outbreak of hostilities in 1642. According to him, 'our late civil warres wholie frustrated' the plans for his legal future. Like most Welshmen, Vaughan was strongly Royalist, and seems for a time to have served with the King's forces. His *Elegie on the death of Mr. R. W. slain in the late unfortunate differences at Rowton Heath, neer Chester, 1645*, contains what reads like an eye-witness account of his friend's prowess in the battle. Another, humorous, poem *Upon a Cloke lent him by Mr. J. Ridsley* also refers to Vaughan's own presence on the scene of the 'differences' at Rowton Heath, and to the time:

> this Jugling fate
> Of Souldierie first seiz'd me!

It is not known when Vaughan began to practise medicine; but in 1673 he wrote from Brecon telling his cousin Aubrey, the antiquary, that he had been a physician 'for many years with good successe . . . & a repute big enough for a person of greater parts than my selfe'. He died in 1695, and was buried in his birthplace, where his grave in the churchyard may still be seen.

Vaughan's first book of poems was published the same year as Crashaw's *Steps to the Temple* appeared. *Poems, with the tenth Satyre of Juvenal Englished* (1646) contains a number of love poems addressed to Amoret (sometimes identified with Vaughan's first wife, Catherine Wise). These are conventionally fashionable songs, of tears and sighs, a cruel fair one with 'a Womans easie Faith', and a young man dying of love. Echoes, here, from Vaughan's contemporaries Habington and Randolph, recur in his later secular volumes, with others from Cartwright and Owen Felltham's *Resolves*. Still more obvious is the borrowing from Donne, especially from *A Valediction: forbidding mourning* (compare the fourth and fifth stanzas of that poem with the third and fourth of Vaughan's *To Amoret, of the difference 'twixt him, and other Lovers, and what true Love is*, and also with the penultimate couplet of *To Amoret gone from him*).

Vaughan's second collection of secular verse, *Olor Iscanus*, followed in 1651. From the date of its dedication, only a year after the appearance of his first book, it seems that publication had been postponed for some time, and that finally much that Vaughan had originally intended to publish had been withdrawn. The publisher's Preface affirms that 'The Author had long agoe condemn'd these Poems to Obscuritie'. Vaughan's reticence, perhaps partly due to the political uncertainties of the later 1640s, possibly owed still more to the profound influence exerted on his whole habit of mind by his discovery of Herbert. This deepening seriousness led him, in his Preface to *Silex Scintillans*, published the previous year, to deplore in vigorous terms his contemporaries' 'inexcusable desertion of *pious sobriety*' in their taste for '*vicious verse*', '*lascivious fictions*' and '*idle books*', and to announce that he himself had 'supprest [his] *greatest follies*'.

The title poem in *Olor Iscanus* celebrates the '*lov'd Arbours*' and '*green banks* and *streams*' of the Usk. The book contains verses to various friends, and in praise of the work of admired writers, including Fletcher, Cartwright, Davenant, and Katherine Philips, the 'wittie fair one' known to her circle as 'the matchless Orinda'. There are verse translations from Ovid, Ausonius, Boethius, and the Polish poet

Casimir, and some in prose from Plutarch and other writers. (Throughout the 1650s Vaughan was publishing prose works such as *The Mount of Olives*, a manual of meditation and prayer free from the 'fruitlesse curiosities of Schoole-Divinity'; or *Flores Solitudinis*, 'collected in his Sicknesse and Retirement', which contained three translations and a biography of St. Paulinus of Nola.)

The third volume of Vaughan's secular poems, *Thalia Rediviva*, sub-titled 'The Pass-times and Diversions of a Countrey-Muse', was published in 1678 (although it contained work of much earlier date). Apart from further translations, and a group of not very remarkable love poems addressed to 'Etesia', there are several religious pieces in the mood of *Silex Scintillans*, probably written after the second part of that collection appeared in 1655. Some of these, *Looking back*, *The Recovery*, and the opening of *The World*, depart from the eight- or ten-syllable couplets favoured by Vaughan in his secular poems to share the greater metrical flexibility and variety of the work in *Silex Scintillans*. The last poem in *Thalia Rediviva*, entitled *Daphnis*, an 'Elegiac Eclogue' between two shepherds, was possibly first written for the death in 1648 of Vaughan's younger brother William, and afterwards adapted for that, in 1666, of Thomas, his twin.

According to their mutual friend Dr. Thomas Powell, Henry and Thomas Vaughan resembled each other as closely in spirit as in body. 'Not only your *faces*,' he declared, 'but your *wits* are *Twins*.' Certainly there are striking parallels between passages in the prose writings of Thomas Vaughan and such poems by his brother as *Regeneration*, *Resurrection and Immortality*, *Vanity of Spirit*, *Corruption*, and *Cock-crowing*. After his eviction from his living in 1650, Thomas Vaughan studied alchemy, and is described by Anthony à Wood as 'a great chymist, a noted son of the fire, an experimental philosopher'. Under the name of Eugenius Philalethes, he published a number of alchemical and mystical treatises which owe much to Hermeticism, the occult philosophy which originated in Greek texts attributed to Hermes Trismegistus. Hermetic traditions, both philosophical and scientific, exercised a powerful attraction for the seventeenth-century mind. The poetry of Donne, for example, and the prose of Sir Thomas Browne, abound in Hermetic allusions—to elixirs, tinctures, essences, influences, and signatures—and in *Religio Medici*, Browne defines death in alchemical terms. This Hermetic interest is plainly recognizable in the work of Henry Vaughan: not only in his translations of two treatises by Nollius, published as *Hermetical Physick* (1655) and *The Chymist's Key* (1657), expounding the medical aspects of Hermetic doctrine, but also in images and ideas found in the symbolism of *Vanity of Spirit, Cock-crowing, The Night, The World, The Constellation,* and *Resurrection and Immortality*. On the whole, however, the imagery in *Silex Scintillans* carries many more echoes both of Herbert, and of biblical language and allusion, than of Hermetic ideas. Essentially Vaughan's are Christian poems which Hermetic terms and notions sometimes furnished with analogies, both apt for his purpose and familiar to contemporary readers, to illustrate the apprehensions of spiritual reality he sought to communicate.[1]

What is the nature of the experience embodied by *Silex Scintillans?* Despite the all-pervading influence of Herbert, this is the work (first published in 1650 and, in a new edition with a second part added, in 1655) which assures Vaughan his secure and permanent place among English religious poets. In it two contrasting themes are clearly defined. One is that of a desolating sense of separation from God through man's sin, which fills the poet with self-disgust and despair; the other, joy in the Presence that animates and illumines all creation, itself visible proof of His power and love.

In his vein of distaste for human life, Vaughan sees earthly existence as a

---

[1] Ross Garner, in *Henry Vaughan: Experience and the Tradition* (1959), gives in Chapter III a useful summary of the relative importance of Hermeticism in Vaughan's work.

> sad captivity,
> This leaden state, which men miscal
> Being and life, but is dead thrall.
>
> (*The Ass*)

The imprisoned spirit 'truly hates to be detained on earth'; and in *Love-sick* Vaughan complains that:

> These narrow skies . . .
> So barre me in, that I am still at warre,
> At constant warre with them.

All through Vaughan's work recurs the desire to escape, 'winged and free', into the 'true liberty' of heaven.

And not only is man a prisoner on earth, he is an exile, banished from home and for ever pining for it:

> He knows he hath a home, but scarce knows where,
> He sayes it is so far
> That he hath quite forgot how to go there.
>
> (*Man*)

The poem *Corruption* relates how he 'came (condemned,) hither,' and

> sigh'd for *Eden*, and would often say
> *Ah! what bright days were those?*

In a world variously referred to as 'wilde woods', parching desert, and wilderness, the spirit yearns with nostalgia:

> O how I long to travell back
> And tread again that ancient track!
>
> (*The Retreate*)

The nature of the place from which man is shut out is memorably epitomized in *Peace*:

> My Soul, there is a Countrie
> Far beyond the stars . . .
> If thou canst get but thither,
> There grows the flowre of peace,
> The Rose that cannot wither,
> Thy fortresse, and thy ease.

Much preoccupied with the cause of this exile from grace, Vaughan views with loathing 'the mule, unruly man', whose body is a 'quicken'd masse of sinne'. Repeatedly the flesh is denounced in such terms as vile, foul, obscene: 'impure, rebellious clay', 'all filth, and spott'. This uncleanness, which obscures the light and alienates man from God, evokes from Vaughan the impassioned cry:

> O that I were all Soul! that thou
> > Wouldst make each part
> Of this poor, sinfull frame pure heart!
> > (*Chearfulness*)

But although in moods of world-weariness and self-disgust Vaughan aspired to an impossible ideal of 'man all pure love, flesh a star', he did not share the Hermetic view of matter as intrinsically evil. Many poems make clear that, for him, the source of sin and separation lies not in the body itself, but in the 'dark Confusions' it houses, which 'soyl thy Temple with a sinful rust' (*Dressing*). Vaughan blames the weakness and waywardness resulting from man's apostasy: his 'black self-wil' and 'sinfull ease', the peevish stubbornness, disobedience and rebellion of his 'hard, stonie heart'.

Abundant proof that Vaughan did not despise material substance as such lies in his frank and lyrical delight in the universe. He saw the wonders of nature body forth the goodness of God, whose 'glory through the world dost drive', and all creation actively proclaim Him:

> There's not a *Spring*,
> Or *Leafe* but hath his *Morning-hymn;* Each *Bush*
> And *Oak* doth know *I AM;*
>
> > (*Rules and Lessons*)

and, in *The Morning-watch*:

> In what Rings,
> And *Hymning Circulations* the quick world
> > Awakes, and sings;
> > The rising winds,

And falling springs,
Birds, beasts, all things
Adore him in their kinds.
Thus all is hurl'd
In sacred *Hymnes*, and *Order*, The great *Chime*
And *Symphony* of nature.

That 'All things here shew [man] heaven . . . and point
him the way home' is, to Vaughan, their ultimate justification. Visible, finite beauty is a bridge to the invisible,
infinite, and transcendent one it symbolizes. The 'Heraldrie/
Of stones, and speechless Earth' shows us our 'true descent'
(*Retirement*); the 'weaker glories' of 'some *gilded Cloud*, or
flowre' intimate to the gazing child 'Some shadows of
eternity' (*The Retreate*). God's 'wondrous Method' in
creating the universe is, in short, the outward proof and
pledge of His omnipresence:

Thou canst not misse his Praise; Each *tree, herb, flowre*
Are shadows of his *wisdome*, and his Pow'r.
(*Rules and Lessons*)

It is here that Vaughan differs most from Herbert, in whose
work nature is little more than a convenient source of telling
metaphor; whereas Vaughan's conception of it is central
to his religious belief. In the plan of creation he perceived a
marvellous unity of design, in which the ordering of natural
phenomena was echoed and repeated in the patterns of man's
spiritual processes. In all of it, as he says in *The Book*,
Vaughan 'lov'd and sought [God's] face'.

'No one else among Donne's followers', affirms Joan
Bennett in *Four Metaphysical Poets*, 'watched the earth, sky
and water, the birds and flowers with the same emotion, nor
with the same delicacy of observation'. This loving pre-
cision of eye and felicity of phrase may be seen in Vaughan's
descriptions of a spring path '*Primros'd*, and hung with
shade', of snow that '*Candies* our Countries wooddy brow',
or of the 'purling Corn'; in a glimpse of dawn:

> I see a Rose
> Bud in the bright East, and disclose
> The Pilgrim-Sunne . . .
>
> (*The Search*)

or of stars that 'nod and sleepe, / And through the dark aire spin a firie thread'; of 'man [as] such a Marygold . . . That shuts, and hangs the head'. One of Vaughan's favourite images for the soul is that of a flower or plant. 'Surly winds', he says in *Regeneration*, 'Blasted my infant buds'; and, in *The Morning-watch*:

> with what flowres,
> And shoots of glory, my soul breakes, and buds!

'True hearts', Vaughan believed, 'spread, and heave/Unto their God, as flow'rs do to the Sun'. Sometimes they send out 'Bright *shootes* of everlastingnesse' (this image of shoots recurs in several poems); but at others, shaken by the storms of sin, the spirit is a 'sully'd flowre', a 'sapless Blossom' thirsting for dew and, at worst, a 'frail' or 'thankless' weed.

E. K. Chambers has said, in his Preface to *The Poems of Henry Vaughan, Silurist* (1896), that Vaughan 'is very much the poet of fine lines and stanzas, of imaginative intervals'; that in a number of poems he begins well and tails off, or else 'some very flinty ground yields a quite unanticipated spark'. The truth of this has to be admitted. Many of Vaughan's poems of conventional religious sentiment are as commonplace as the average hymn, unlit by any memorable flash of poetic insight or language. Vaughan can be—as in *Church Service*, *The Passion*, *Tears*, *Holy Scriptures*, *The Relapse*, or the jogtrot jingle of 'Thou that know'st for whom I mourne'—disconcertingly trite and sententious, even banal. He has, compared with Herbert, little sense of form or the disciplines of verbal economy. But there are whole poems—*The Retreate*, *The Morning-watch*, *Peace*, *Affliction*, *Man*, 'They are all gone into the world of light!'—which do sustain a high poetic level; and for the isolated splendours,

where (in Vaughan's own image) the flint does strike off
sparks, how luminous some of these are!

> I saw Eternity the other night
> Like a great *Ring* of pure and endless light,
>   All calm, as it was bright,
> And round beneath it, Time in hours, days, years
>   Driv'n by the spheres
> Like a vast shadow mov'd, in which the world
>   And all her train were hurl'd;
>
> (The World)

or:

> There is in God (some say)
> A deep, but dazling darkness . . .
> O for that night! where I in him
> Might live invisible and dim.
>
> (The Night)

or his apostrophe, in 'They are all gone into the world
of light!', of

> Dear, beauteous death! the Jewel of the Just,
>   Shining nowhere, but in the dark,

and, from the same poem:

> It glows and glitters in my cloudy brest
> Like stars upon some gloomy grove . . .

All these lodge in the imagination with the unforgettable
impact, the haunting inevitability, of pure poetry.

It will be noticed how many of these magical lines
enshrine images of *light*. Present in many contexts, light
glows through and permeates all Vaughan's work. His books
are 'Burning and shining Thoughts'. Man before the Fall
was as 'intimate with Heav'n, as light'. The saints,

> Like Candles, shed
> Their beams, and light
> Us into Bed,

while the dead walk

> in an Air of glory,
> Whose light doth trample on my days.

Imploring 'The beams, and brightnes of thy face', the poet appeals to God to

> brush me with thy light, that I
> May shine unto a perfect day;

and aspires towards a state where he may

> Rove in that mighty, and eternall light
> Where no rude shade, or night
> Shall dare approach us.

For Vaughan light is the primary symbol of spiritual illumination, of that clarity and purity of vision man possessed most fully when he 'Shin'd in [his] Angell-infancy'.

Two human conditions, Vaughan believed, enable the achievement of this illumination at its steadiest and most radiant. One (as already seen) is in man's attunement to natural beauty in constant awareness of its being divinely infused:

> . . . *rural shades* are the sweet fense
> Of piety and innocence . . .
> If *Eden* be on Earth at all,
> 'Tis that, which we the *Country* call.
>
> (*Retirement*)

The other state of being which, in Vaughan's view, is the habitation of angels and reflects the image of Eden, is our early years of innocence: that

> first, happy age;
> An age without distast and warrs,

as he sees it in *Looking back;* and, in *Childe-hood*, as the

> Dear, harmless age! the short, swift span,
> Where weeping virtue parts with man.

Leaving infancy behind, man finds that, amid the world's insistent claims and clamour, sin has 'Like Clouds ecclips'd [his] mind':

> I find my selfe the lesse, the more I grow;
>   The world
> Is full of voices; Man is call'd, and hurl'd
>   By each, he answers all.
>
> (Distraction)

The completest embodiment of Vaughan's belief in the sanctity of childhood experience is *The Retreate*, a poem which has sometimes been regarded as one of the germinative influences on Wordsworth's *Ode on the Intimations of Immortality*. Although this is not established, the two poets certainly share the same nostalgic reverence for the vision of those years when, according to Wordsworth:

> trailing clouds of glory do we come
> From God, who is our home:
> Heaven lies about us in our infancy!

and, in the words of Vaughan:

> Happy those early dayes! when I
> Shin'd in my Angell-infancy.
> Before I understood this place
> Appointed for my second race,
> Or taught my soul to fancy ought
> But a white, Celestiall thought,
> When yet I had not walkt above
> A mile, or two, from my first love,
> And looking back (at that short space,)
> Could see a glimpse of his bright-face;
> When on some *gilded Cloud*, or *flowre*
> My gazing soul would dwell an houre,
> And in those weaker glories spy
> Some shadows of eternity;

> Before I taught my tongue to wound
> My Conscience with a sinfull sound,
> Or had the black art to dispence
> A sev'rall sinne to ev'ry sence,
> But felt through all this fleshly dresse
> Bright *shootes* of everlastingnesse.

The phrase 'first love', or 'early love', recurs with peculiar poignancy in different poems—*Corruption, The Constellation, The Seed growing secretly*—for man's relation with God. In the same way the idea of angels, walking and talking as man's familiars, is one of Vaughan's favourite symbols—as in *Religion, Corruption, The Jews, Childe-hood* and *Retirement*—to convey his conception of our lost Eden. A return to the state of mind, heart, and spirit known in childhood is, Vaughan believed, the way back to that original fullness of communion between man and his Creator:

> Some men a forward motion love,
> But I by backward steps would move,
> And when this dust falls to the urn
> In that state I came return.

HENRY VAUGHAN

Select Bibliography

BIBLIOGRAPHIES

MARILLA, ESMOND L. *A Comprehensive Bibliography of Henry Vaughan*. University of Alabama Press, 1948.

—— and J. D. SIMMONDS. *Henry Vaughan: A Bibliographical Supplement, 1946–1960*. University of Alabama Press, 1963.

MARTIN, LEONARD C., ed. *The Works*. 2nd ed. Oxford: Clarendon Press, 1957.
Contains a bibliography.

SOME COLLECTED EDITIONS

The Sacred Poems and Private Ejaculations. London: Pickering, 1847; Boston: Little, Brown, 1854.

The Complete Works in Verse and Prose. Edited by Alexander B. Grosart. Fuller Worthies' Library. 4 vols. Blackburn, Lancashire: Privately Printed, 1871.

The Poems. Edited by Edmund K. Chambers. Muses' Library. 2 vols. London: Lawrence and Bullen, 1896.

The Works. 2nd ed. Edited by Leonard C. Martin (see above).
The standard edition, with a bibliography and a biography. Contains additions and corrections to the first edition, 1914.

The Secular Poems. Edited by Esmond L. Marilla. Cambridge: Harvard University Press, 1958.

Poetry and Selected Prose. Edited by Leonard C. Martin. Oxford Standard Authors. New York: Oxford University Press, 1963.
Based on the editor's standard full edition, with translations of the Latin poems.

SEPARATE WORKS
Dates of original editions are given.

Poems, with the Tenth Satire of Juvenal Englished. London, 1646.

Silex Scintillans: Sacred Poems and Private Ejaculations. London, 1650.

Olor Iscanus: Select Poems and Translations. London, 1651.

The Mount of Olives: or Solitary Devotions. London, 1652.

Flores Solitudinis: Collected in his Sickness and Retirement. London, 1654. Prose translations.

Hermetical Physic. London, 1655.
A translation of Nollius' *Systema Medicinae Hermeticae Generale.*

The Chymist's Key. London, 1657.
A translation of Nollius' *De Generatione.*

Thalia Rediviva: The Pastimes and Diversions of a Country Muse, in choice Poems on several Occasions. With some learned Remains of Eugenius Philalethes [i.e., Vaughan's twin, Thomas]. London, 1678.

BIOGRAPHICAL AND CRITICAL STUDIES OF VAUGHAN

HODGSON, GERALDINE E. *A Study in Illumination.* London: Heath, Cranton, Ouseley, 1914.

HOLMES, ELIZABETH. *Henry Vaughan and the Hermetic Philosophy.* Oxford: Blackwell, 1932.

MARTIN, LEONARD C. "Henry Vaughan and the Theme of Infancy," *Seventeenth Century Studies Presented to Sir Herbert Grierson.* Oxford: Clarendon Press, 1938.

HUTCHINSON, FRANCIS E. *Henry Vaughan: A Life and Interpretation.* Oxford: Clarendon Press, 1947.
The standard biography.

GARNER, ROSS. *Henry Vaughan: Experience and the Tradition.* Chicago: University of Chicago Press, 1959.

PETTET, E. C. *Of Paradise and Light: A Study of Vaughan's* Silex Scintillans. Cambridge: University Press, 1960.

OLSON, PAUL A. "Vaughan's *The World:* The Pattern of Meaning and the Tradition," *Comparative Literature,* XIII (1961).

DURR, R. A. *On The Mystical Poetry of Henry Vaughan.* Cambridge: Harvard University Press, 1962.

GARNER, ROSS. *The Unprofitable Servant in Henry Vaughan.* University of Nebraska Studies No. 29 (N.S.). Lincoln, 1963.

THOMAS TRAHERNE

by Margaret Willy

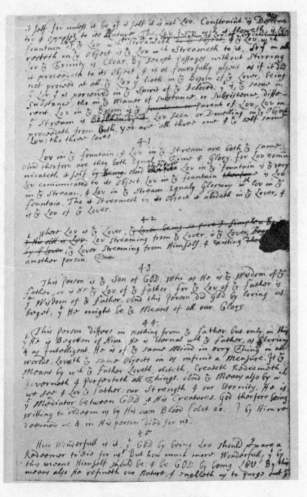

THOMAS TRAHERNE

Page of Ms. from *The Centuries of Meditation*. By the kind permission of the Clarendon Press, Oxford.

Thomas Traherne was born in Hereford about 1637. He died in September or early October 1674 at Teddington, Middlesex.

THOMAS TRAHERNE

Just over half a century ago two unsigned manuscript note-books, one in prose, the other verse, were discovered on a London bookstall. First ascribed to Vaughan, because of certain resemblances to the style and spirit of his writing, they were finally established as the work of a contemporary, Thomas Traherne.

The original confusion of authorship was understandable. A strong vein of mysticism runs through the writing of both Vaughan and Traherne—one a Welshman, the other born on the borders of Wales. There are similarities in vocabulary as well as in verse-forms. But the most striking affinity lies in their common attitude towards childhood. Vaughan's thought in *The Retreate* is vividly paralleled by Traherne's writing, both in verse and prose, about early experience. Everything then, says Traherne, seemed to have "been made but to Day Morning", and was seen with the eyes of an angel or the first man:

> Certainly Adam in Paradise had not more sweet and curious apprehensions of the World, than I when I was a child.

> I was Entertained like an Angel with the Works of GOD in their Splendour and Glory; I saw all in the Peace of Eden; Heaven and Earth did sing my Creators Praises and could not make more Melody to Adam, then to me.[1]

In the poem *Eden* Traherne recalls that

> Only what Adam in his first Estate,
> Did I behold . . .

> Those things which first his Eden did adorn,
>   My Infancy
> Did crown.

For Traherne, as for Vaughan, 'The first Impressions are Immortal all' (*Dumnesse*); the purity of infant intuitions the key to life's most fundamental realities, a mystery 'which the Books of the Learned never unfold':

> Those Pure and Virgin Apprehensions I had from the Womb, and that Divine Light wherewith I was born are the Best unto this Day . . . Verily they seem the Greatest Gifts His Wisdom could bestow, for without them all other Gifts had been Dead and Vain.[1]

We see Vaughan, in the poem *Childe-hood*, aspiring to re-capture the unique quality of that early vision:

> I cannot reach it; and my striving eye
> Dazles at it, as at eternity,

and apostrophizing the 'age of mysteries':

> How do I study now, and scan
> Thee, more then ere I studyed man.

In the same way Traherne, throughout his adult life, re-garded it as the first duty of a man to regain that wisdom, 'unattainable by Book', which informs our childhood appre-hensions of a world beyond the visible one. The felicity possible for all human beings could, he believed, be achieved by deliberately and diligently cultivating the innocence of the 'Infant-Ey', and 'becom[ing] as it were a little Child again.'[1]

The son of a shoemaker, Thomas Traherne was born, about 1637, in Hereford. He was brought up by well-to-do relatives; and it was almost certainly through the provision of his uncle, Philip Traherne, a prosperous innkeeper and twice Mayor of Hereford City, that Thomas, in his fif-teenth year, went to Oxford, the first in a family of farmers and tradesmen to achieve the distinction of a university

[1]*Centuries of Meditations.*

education. His zestful pursuit of his studies, which he describes in *Centuries of Meditations*, his intellectual curiosity and
eagerness to explore the individual mysteries and whole
nature of the universe, were typical of the spirit of his age.

Like Crashaw, Traherne made a deliberate choice of the
'little contentfull kingdom' of celibacy and study. At the
end of 1657, having resolved

> to Spend [all my Time] whatever it cost me, in Search of
> Happiness . . . [choosing] rather to live upon 10 pounds a yeer,
> and to go in Lether Clothes, and feed upon Bread and Water,
> so that I might have all my time clearly to my self . . .
>
> (*III Century*: 46)

he went as Rector to the parish of Credenhill, near Hereford.
There, with intervals of absence at Oxford, Traherne lived
the simple, but for him deeply satisfying, life of an obscure
country parson; until, in 1667, he went to London as private
chaplain to Sir Orlando Bridgeman, Charles II's Lord
Keeper of the Seal. Traherne remained in Sir Orlando's
service until 1674, the year of his patron's death and, a few
months later, at the same early age as Crashaw, of his own.
Opening up far wider horizons to one who was, on his own
admission, 'a sociable Creature . . . a lover of company',
and thereby enlarging and enriching his terms of reference,
these last seven years were of immense benefit to the
vitality of Traherne's work.

His writings cannot be placed in any certain order of
composition. The only book to be published in his lifetime
was *Roman Forgeries*, which appeared in 1673, anonymously,
but with a bold dedication to Traherne's patron, by now
disgraced and deprived of office. This was one more instal-
ment in the ceaseless religious controversy between the
Anglican Church and Rome; and its author accused 'the
Pope's sworn Adjutants' of forging early Church records.
Its interest today is slight; but it does reveal something of
Traherne's formidable intellectual capacity—both the scope

of his scholarship and the clarity and incisiveness of his argument.

Christian Ethicks, dispatched to its publisher immediately before Traherne's death, appeared posthumously the following year. It was a treatise on human conduct, a discussion of morality with a difference; for, unlike many contemporary writers on ethics, Traherne was little concerned with castigating vice, being 'entirely taken up with the Worth and Beauty of Virtue'. A protest against the materialism of Hobbes's *Leviathan* (1651), the book is an impassioned and eloquent exposition both of the reality of spiritual values and of Traherne's personal creed of joy—what he called 'Christian epicureanism'. Structurally *Christian Ethicks* is rambling and unco-ordinated; but as a record of inner adventure and discovery, written out of the knowledge its author 'gained in the nature of *Felicity* by many years earnest and diligent study', it is an impressive piece of spiritual autobiography.

In 1699 there appeared, again anonymously, the book of devotions with a cumbersome title (probably not the author's own) which is generally known simply as *Thanksgivings*. These are a series of prose-poems in gratitude for such benefits as 'The Glory of God's Works' and 'The Wisdom of his Word', carrying echoes of the *Devotions* of Lancelot Andrewes and, in their rhythms and re-iterations, of the Psalms. In the exuberant outpouring of synonymous phrases, the incantatory piling up of images in freely flowing, flexible lines, and their sense of soaring, triumphant vitality, these 'rapturous tumbling catalogue[s] of delights and interests' (as 'Q' described them) convey the impression that the writer can scarcely contain his exultation: being 'in danger of bursting, till we can communicate all to some fit and amiable recipient, and more delight in Communication than we did in the Reception'.[1] A sense of urgent, impetuous motion is as characteristic of Traherne's writing as its

---

[1] *Christian Ethicks.*

quality of radiance diffused through images of light ('Pure Primitive Virgin Light', 'burning Ardent fire', 'Glorious Rayes', 'Shining Beams'), for which he has a fondness almost equalling Vaughan's.

A Collection of Meditations and Devotions in Three Parts, which appeared in 1717, also apparently belongs to Traherne's Credenhill years. The first part, *Hexameron,* or *Meditations on the Six Days of Creation,* has the same energy and sense of the wonderful diversity of life which characterizes the *Thanksgivings.* The second, *Meditations and Devotions upon the Life of Christ,* contains many incidental passages of self-revelation: in particular, misgivings about personal faults and failures, fluctuations of mood and faith, and, above all, concerning that desolation of spiritual banishment the writer calls "the dark dismal Destitutions of all Light".

Traherne's poems were not published until the first decade of this century: the first volume in 1903, and a second—which had been prepared by his brother Philip, with assiduous and often disastrous 'revisions', under the title *Poems of Felicity*—in 1910. Traherne employed the heroic couplet or, more frequently, the long, elaborately patterned, irregular stanza. His exaltation of childhood innocence, and perception of its kinship with the mystic's awareness of harmony and happiness, produced some of his best poems, such as *The Salutation,* or the opening of *Wonder:*

> How like an Angel came I down!
>   How Bright are all Things here!
> When first among his Works I did appear
>   O how their GLORY me did Crown!
> The World resembled his ETERNITIE,
>   In which my Soul did Walk;
> And evry Thing that I did see
>   Did with me talk.

In *News* he describes those intimations of immortality which are the child's memories of the place whence he came, their now 'Absent Bliss' beckoning him to its rediscovery.

But Traherne's poetry is, on the whole, far inferior in quality to his prose. There are the scattered felicities, as

> I within did flow
> With Seas of Life like Wine;
>
> (*Wonder*)

or

> Drown'd in their Customs, I became
> A Stranger to the Shining Skies,
> Lost as a dying Flame.
>
> (*The Apostasy*)

But too often the long, cumulative lists of attributes or blessings sprawl, as in the third and fourth stanzas of *Desire*, into trite and repetitive diffuseness. Traherne as a poet lacked the discipline to prune superfluous verbiage, cut out the meaningless, redundant phrase used merely to achieve a rhyme; while the rhyming itself is frequently facile and expected enough to result in a jingle.

Traherne's strength as a writer of prose lay in his equal mastery of two styles, employed according to the subject and purpose of the work in hand. In *Christian Ethicks*, and the energetic argument of *Roman Forgeries*, he rejected what a Royal Society writer of 1644 had impatiently dismissed as the current 'luxury and redundance of speech . . . amplification, digressions, and swellings of style', in favour of short sentences and plain, straightforward exposition. The personal note of frank and easy address to his reader, which is so engaging a feature of nearly all Traherne's prose work, derived largely from Cowley (borrowing in his turn from Montaigne). These new trends in English prose were a reaction against pompous and bombastic 'volubility of Tongue'. But, when occasion demanded, Traherne could command all the dignity and sonorous splendour of the older manner, with its stately rhythms, re-iterations, and antitheses. It is through his successful blend of the vigorous simplicity of the new and rhetorical grandeur of the old

styles with a tone of friendly, familiar discourse, that
Traherne achieves in *Centuries of Meditations* so remarkable
a range and richness of expression.

This book, which after the manuscript's chance discovery
was published in 1908, places Traherne among the masters
of English religious prose. Here, as nowhere else in his
writing, he attained a harmonious fusion of form and content. To compare a passage from *The Centuries* with one of
the *Thanksgivings* will at once show how his earlier stylistic
exuberance has been disciplined by a new economy and
restraint.

Centuries of Meditations was written, as a manual of
instruction in the way of felicity, for a friend (almost
certainly Mrs. Susanna Hopton of Kington, near Credenhill).
This fact partly accounts for its note of intimacy and fullness of self-revelation. For his friend's spiritual guidance
Traherne filled the small leather notebook she had given
him 'with Profitable Wonders . . . Things Strange yet
Common; Incredible, yet known; Most High, yet plain;
infinitly Profitable, but not Esteemed' (*I Century: 1 and 3*).
The manuscript consisted of four complete groups, and part
of a fifth, of a hundred numbered prose sections. In these
we find the inner history of their author's achievement of
happiness; the completest expression of his most profound
religious convictions and philosophy of dedicated joy.
Centuries of Meditations is a testament of praise: those praises
which, Traherne declared, are 'the Marks and Symptoms of a
Happy Life . . . the very End for which the World was
created' (*III Century: 82*).

Nowhere, perhaps, have the feel and flavour of childhood
experience been more vividly recaptured. In his infancy,
Traherne affirms in the second section of the Third *Century*
(and also in the poem *Wonder*), he was oblivious of adult
cares:

> I Knew not that there were any Sins, or Complaints, or Laws.
> I dreamed not of Poverties Contentions or Vices. All Tears and

Quarrels, were hidden from mine Eys. Evry Thing was at Rest, Free, and Immortal. I Knew Nothing of Sickness or Death, or Exaction.

Later, 'the first Light which shined in my Infancy in its Primitive and Innocent Clarity was totally ecclypsed'. Yet before that inevitable loss, and the conflicts of adolescence so convincingly described in poems like *Dissatisfaction* and *Solitude*, despite, too, an early inclination 'secretly to Expostulate with GOD for not giving me Riches' (*III Century:* 14), the picture of childhood felicity shines bright and unflawed. In the magic circle of the self-enclosed, yet limitless, world the child inhabited,

> All appeared New, and Strange at the first, inexpressibly rare, and Delightfull, and Beautifull. I was a little Stranger which at my Enterance into the World was Saluted and Surrounded with innumerable Joys.
>
> (*III Century:* 2)

It is not, of course, as mere straightforward autobiography that we should read Traherne's revelations of his childhood. The child's imaginative preoccupations, such as those of the poem *Shadows in the Water*, or the speculations described in *III Century:* 17 and 18, are intended always to symbolize the spirit's activity in a sphere beyond the everyday material one. 'A man's life of any worth', said Keats, 'is a continual allegory.' It is as an allegory of the adventures of the spirit that Traherne's early life is to be interpreted; the *Centuries* and poems—like Shakespeare's works in Keats's letter—are the comments on it.

The essence of Traherne's apprehension of the child's-eye view of the universe is concentrated in the famous third section of the Third *Century*, beginning:

> The Corn was Orient and Immortal Wheat, which never should be reaped, nor was ever sown. I thought it had stood from everlasting to everlasting. The Dust and Stones of the Street were as Precious as GOLD. The Gates were at first the End of the

World, The Green Trees when I saw them first through one of the Gates Transported and Ravished me; their Sweetness and unusual Beauty made my Heart to leap, and almost mad with Extasie, they were such strange and Wonderfull Thing.

In the subtle shadings of sentence-pattern and gradations of rhythm, which so skilfully communicate the pulse of mounting exultation, this is one of the sublime passages of English prose. Once heard, its majestic, reverberating cadences continue to haunt the imagination and the inward ear.

Three main aspects of Traherne's attitude to life are expressed here. First, there is his exaltation of the child's ignorance of the 'Dirty Devices of this World'. Then there is the sense of wonder which springs direct from that innocence: the freshness and luminous intensity of vision that can transmute the common dust and stones of the street into a substance as precious as gold, turn the tumbling playmates into 'moving Jewels', and cause the very trees to ravish the beholder's eyes and make his heart leap, 'almost mad with Extasie'. Thirdly, and perhaps most potently of all, we are conscious of release into a state of *boundlessness:* of the illimitable horizons, unconfined by either time or space, that Traherne is looking back to praise as the purest of his early joys. For him, then, 'All Time was Eternity, and a Perpetual Sabbath' (*III Century:* 2). It was no ordinary corn, but immortal wheat, that waved in the harvest fields; human life was still unshadowed by mortality ('I knew not that they were Born or should Die'). There was neither beginning nor end in this region where 'Eternity was Manifest in the Light of the Day, and som thing infinit Behind evry thing appeared'. It is in his communication of these world-without-end intimations that Traherne comes nearest to Blake, for whom also it was an 'augury of innocence' to

> Hold Infinity in the palm of your hand
> And Eternity in an hour.

No child is ever actively conscious of being happy:

indeed it is that very freedom from awareness of self, oblivious of the rarity of his state, that is a condition of the child's wonder and freshness of vision. Yet Traherne's pursuit of felicity, in *Centuries of Meditations*, depends largely on an enriching *consciousness* of happiness:

> You never Enjoy the World aright, till you so love the Beauty of Enjoying it, that you are Covetous and Earnest to Persuade others to Enjoy it.
>
> *(I Century:* 31)

Striving to recapture and perpetuate in maturity the timeless joys of infancy, Traherne the man was consciously practising what, as a child, he had unconsciously possessed.

'Enjoy', and 'Enjoyment', are among the most frequent words in *Centuries of Meditations*. It could be said that Traherne was one of the world's great *enjoyers;* and nowhere does this emerge more triumphantly than in the twenty-ninth and thirtieth sections of the First *Century*. These express the passionate conviction of a man who could never have been so joyous a servant of God if he had not first loved the earth's beauty to his fullest capacity as a human being:

> You never Enjoy the World aright, till the Sea it self floweth in your Veins, till you are Clothed with the Heavens, and Crowned with the Stars: and Perceiv your self to be the Sole Heir of the whole World: and more then so, becaus Men are in it who are evry one Sole Heirs, as well as you. Till you can Sing and Rejoyce and Delight in GOD, as Misers do in Gold, and Kings in Scepters, you never Enjoy the World.
>
> Till your Spirit filleth the whole World, and the Stars are your Jewels, till you are as Familiar with the Ways of God in all Ages as with your Walk and Table . . . you never Enjoy the World.

And it was not only the immensities of sea, sky, and stars which were Traherne's objects of enjoyment and, therefore, of worship. We are reminded of Blake's grain of sand in the opening of the twenty-seventh section of the First *Century:*

> You never Enjoy the World aright, till you see how a Sand
> Exhibiteth the Wisdom and Power of God.

Nothing was too small or insignificant to minister to this
man's delight and call forth his praise; from such familiar
daily blessings as the 'lovly lively air', the 'Precious Jewel' of
a waterdrop, and 'evry Spire of Grass', to the diverse
personalities of men and women, who are, he affirms in
III Century: 22, 'when well understood a Principal Part of
of our True felicity'. Traherne rejoiced in everything from
the simple fulfilment of his material needs—bread, meat and
drink, his clothes, fuel, and 'Household stuff, Books,
Utensils, Furniture'—to the intricate mechanism of the
human body (*I Century*: 66) and the treasures of art.

If, in brief, Traherne's eyes were for the most part fixed
on things beyond this earth, his feet were always firmly
planted upon it. His appetite for enjoyment was wonder-
fully comprehensive. He saw the gift of human existence
framed that man might taste both the sensuous pleasure of
the animals and the spiritual ecstasy of the angels. To be
satisfied as God is, he declares in the First *Century*, men must
first want like gods: for 'Infinit Want is the very Ground
and Caus of infinit Treasure'.

To despise and dismiss the divinely planned pattern of
the earth seemed to Traherne a sin against man's potential-
ities for praise; an 'abominable corruption' of his nature
which denied that 'heavenly Avarice' implanted in him as
positive proof of his immortal soul and its destination. And
so the universe became for him the 'Book from Heaven' he
had demanded in adolescence: a book in whose pages he
constantly read the power and love of its Author. Traherne
did, however, perceive the necessity for disciplining sensuous enjoyment through dedicating it. The senses could
never, to him, be more than, in the metaphor of *News*,
ambassadors bringing tidings from a foreign country
which housed his true treasure. Men are spiritual, Traherne

believed, according to the degree in which they esteem and enjoy their temporal gifts:

> Wine by its Moysture quencheth my Thirst, whether I consider it or no: but to see it flowing from his Lov who gav it unto Man Quencheth the Thirst even of the Holy Angels. To consider it, is to Drink it Spiritualy.

In that last sentence lies the core of Traherne's philosophy. To *consider*, and in doing so, to praise: thus, for the contemplative man, could the everyday pleasures of sense be perpetually sanctified.

It was this capacity for enjoying the world on two planes, natural and transcendental—for extracting, here and now, the essence from temporal delight while simultaneously viewing it *sub specie aeternitatis* — which made Thomas Traherne 'Felicity's perfect lover'. For him indeed:

> Life! Life [was] all: in its most full extent
> Stretcht out to all things, and with all Content!

THOMAS TRAHERNE

Select Bibliography

BIBLIOGRAPHY

WADE, GLADYS I. *Thomas Traherne: A Critical Biography*. Princeton: Princeton University Press, 1944; reprinted, 1946.
Contains a bibliography.

COLLECTED EDITION

Thomas Traherne: Centuries, Poems, and Thanksgivings. Edited by Herschel M. Margoliouth. 2 vols. Oxford: Clarendon Press, 1958.
The standard edition.

SEPARATE WORKS
Dates of original editions are given, and some modern editions are also recorded here.

Roman Forgeries, by a Faithful Son of the Church of England. London, 1673.

Christian Ethics. London, 1675.
Modernised as *The Way To Blessedness* by Margaret Bottrall (London: Faith, 1962).

A Serious and Pathetical Contemplation of the Mercies of God, in Several Most Devout and Sublime Thanksgivings for the Same. London, 1699.
Published anonymously. Edited by Roy Daniells (Toronto: University of Toronto Press, 1941).

A Collection of Meditations and Devotions in Three Parts. London, 1717.

The Poetical Works, now First Published, from the Original Manuscripts. Edited by Bertram Dobell. London: Dobell, 1903; 3rd ed., edited by Gladys I. Wade, 1932.

Centuries of Meditation, now First Printed from the Author's Manuscript. Edited by Bertram Dobell. London: Dobell, 1908.
Edited with an introduction by John Farrar (New York: Harper, 1960).

Poems of Felicity. Edited by Harold I. Bell. Oxford: Clarendon Press, 1910. Contains thirty-nine poems in addition to those first edited by Dobell in 1903.

Of Magnanimity and Chastity. Edited by John R. Slater. New York: King's Crown Press, 1942.

BIOGRAPHICAL AND CRITICAL STUDIES OF TRAHERNE

WILLETT, GLADYS. *Traherne*. Cambridge: Heffer, 1919.

IREDALE, HILDA. *Thomas Traherne*. Oxford: Blackwell, 1935.

WADE, GLADYS I. *Thomas Traherne: A Critical Biography* (see above). Contains the fullest existing biography of the poet, and a detailed examination of his individual writings.

GENERAL CRITICAL STUDIES
OF METAPHYSICAL POETRY

Select Bibliography

This list takes no account of the important early criticism of, for example, Dryden (see especially "The Original and Progress of Satire"), Johnson (see especially "The Life of Abraham Cowley"), and Coleridge (see especially *Biographia Literaria*), or of the lives of Herbert and Donne by Isaak Walton—in *Lives of Donne and Herbert,* edited by S. C. Roberts (Cambridge: University Press, 1928).

GRIERSON, HERBERT J. C. *The First Half of the Seventeenth Century*. New York: Charles Scribner's Sons, 1906.

ELIOT, T. S. "The Metaphysical Poets," *The Times Literary Supplement* (1921).
Reprinted in *Selected Essays* (New York: Harcourt, Brace & World, 1932; new enlarged edition, 1950), and in William R. Keast, *Seventeenth-Century English Poetry* (see below). Eliot's essays on Massinger (in *Selected Essays*), and on Milton—*Essays and Studies by Members of the English Association,* XXI (1936), and *Milton* (London: Oxford University Press, 1948)—are also relevant.

LOUDON, K. M. *Two Mystic Poets*. Oxford: Blackwell, 1922.
On Crashaw and Vaughan.

PRAZ, MARIO. *Secentismo e Marinismo in Inghilterra: John Donne—Richard Crashaw*. Florence: La Voce, 1925.

GRIERSON, HERBERT J. C. *Cross Currents in English Literature of the XVIIth Century*. London: Chatto and Windus, 1929.

BENNETT, JOAN. *Four Metaphysical Poets: Donne, Herbert, Vaughan, and Crashaw*. Cambridge: University Press, 1934; 2nd ed., 1953.

LEISHMAN, JAMES B. *The Metaphysical Poets: Donne, Herbert, Vaughan, Traherne*. Oxford: Clarendon Press, 1934; New York: Russell and Russell, 1963.

WILLEY, BASIL. *The Seventeenth Century Background.* London: Chatto and Windus, 1934.

LEAVIS, F. R. "English Poetry in the Seventeenth Century," *Scrutiny,* IV (1935).
See also "The Line of Wit" in Leavis's *Revaluation* (London: Chatto and Windus, 1936); reprinted in William R. Keast, *Seventeenth-Century English Poetry* (see below).

WHITE, HELEN C. *The Metaphysical Poets: A Study in Religious Experience.* New York: Macmillan, 1936.

PRAZ, MARIO. *Studies in Seventeenth-Century Imagery.* 2 vols. London: Warburg Institute, 1939–1948.

SHARP, ROBERT L. *From Donne to Dryden: The Revolt against Metaphysical Poetry.* Chapel Hill: University of North Carolina Press, 1940.

BUSH, DOUGLAS. *English Literature in the Earlier Seventeenth Century.* Oxford: Clarendon Press, 1945.

TUVE, ROSEMOND. *Elizabethan and Metaphysical Imagery: Renaissance Poetic and Twentieth-Century Critics.* Chicago: University of Chicago Press, 1947.
The most important landmark in postwar Donne criticism.

FREEMAN, ROSEMARY. *English Emblem Books.* London: Chatto and Windus, 1948.

WALLERSTEIN, RUTH. *Studies in Seventeenth-Century Poetic.* Madison: University of Wisconsin Press, 1950.
A difficult but valuable work, to be read in conjunction with Tuve (see above).

NICOLSON, MARJORIE HOPE. *The Breaking of the Circle: Studies in the Effect of the "New Science" upon Seventeenth Century Poetry.* Evanston: Northwestern University Press, 1950; rev. ed., New York: Columbia University Press, 1960.

WEDGWOOD, C. V. *Seventeenth-Century English Literature.* New York: Oxford University Press, 1950.
An introductory volume.

MAZZEO, J. A. "A Seventeenth-Century Theory of Metaphysical Poetry," *Romanic Review,* XLII (1951).

———. "A Critique of some Modern Theories of Metaphysical Poetry," *Modern Philology,* L (1952).
Reprinted in William R. Keast, *Seventeenth-Century English Poetry* (see below).

———. "Metaphysical Poetry and the Poetic of Correspondence," *Journal of the History of Ideas*, XIV (1953).

DUNCAN, JOSEPH E. "The Revival of Metaphysical Poetry, 1872–1912," *PMLA*, LXVIII (1953).

BETHELL, S. L. "Gracian, Tesauro, and the Nature of Metaphysical Wit," *The Northern Miscellany of Literary Criticism*, I (1953).

MARTZ, LOUIS. *The Poetry of Meditation: A Study in English Literature of the Seventeenth Century*. Yale Studies in English No. 125. New Haven: Yale University Press, 1954; rev. ed., 1962.

SMITH, A. J. "An Examination of Some Claims for Ramism," *Review of English Studies*, VII (N.S.) (1956).

FORD, BORIS, ed. *From Donne to Marvell*. Pelican Guide to English Literature Vol. 3. Baltimore: Penguin, 1956.

DUNCAN, JOSEPH E. *The Revival of Metaphysical Poetry*. Minneapolis: University of Minnesota Press, 1959.

WILLIAMSON, GEORGE. *Seventeenth-Century Contexts*. London: Faber and Faber, 1960.

ELLRODT, ROBERT. *L'Inspiration Personelle et L'Esprit du Temps chez les Poètes Métaphysiques Anglais*. 3 vols. Paris: Corti, 1960.

ALVAREZ, ALFRED. *The School of Donne*. New York: Pantheon, 1962.

KEAST, WILLIAM R. *Seventeenth-Century English Poetry: Modern Essays in Criticism*. A Galaxy Book. New York: Oxford University Press, 1962.
A convenient collection of twenty-seven important critical essays, most of them about metaphysical poetry.

WILLIAMSON, GEORGE. *The Proper Wit of Poetry*. Chicago: University of Chicago Press, 1962.

Note. Further studies and reference works are listed in: *The Cambridge Bibliography of English Literature*, 4 vols. (1941) and *Supplement* (1957); the Annual Bibliographies published in *PMLA* by the Modern Language Association of America; *The Year's Work in English Studies*, a survey of important critical books and articles, published annually for the English Association by Oxford University Press; the *Annual Bibliography of English Language and Literature*, an extensive listing of critical books and articles, published for the Modern Humanities Research Association by Cambridge University Press; and "Literature of the Renaissance," an annual bibliography published in *Studies in Philology* (1917–in progress).

SELECT LIST OF ANTHOLOGIES

GRIERSON, HERBERT J. C., ed. *Metaphysical Lyrics and Poems of the Seventeenth Century*. Oxford: Clarendon Press, 1921.
The prefatory essay constitutes a first-class critical introduction to seventeenth-century metaphysical poetry and is reprinted in William R. Keast, *Seventeenth-Century English Poetry* (see above, p. 143).

AULT, NORMAN, ed. *Seventeenth Century Lyrics*. New York: Longmans, Green, 1928.

GRIERSON, HERBERT J. C. and GEOFFREY BULLOUGH, eds. *The Oxford Book of Seventeenth Century Verse*. Oxford: Clarendon Press, 1934.

HAYWARD, JOHN, ed. *Seventeenth Century Poetry*. London: Chatto and Windus, 1948.

GARDNER, HELEN, ed. *The Metaphysical Poets*. Baltimore: Penguin Books, 1957; New York: Oxford University Press, 1961.
This anthology also contains an illuminating critical introduction.

MARTZ, LOUIS, ed. *The Meditative Poem: An Anthology of Seventeenth-Century Verse*. Anchor Books. Garden City, N. Y.: Doubleday, 1963.
Extensive paperback anthology, with introduction and notes.

RECORDING

17th Century Poetry. Caedmon TC 1049.
Read by Cedric Hardwicke and Robert Newton. Poems by Herbert, Strode, Traherne, Vaughan, Crashaw, Marvell, and others.